T0300332

ROUTLEDGE LIBRARY EDITIONS:
WORK & SOCIETY

Volume 17

THE FIXING OF WAGES IN GOVERNMENT EMPLOYMENT

THE FIXING OF WAGES
IN GOVERNMENT
EMPLOYMENT

E. COLSTON SHEPHERD

LONDON AND NEW YORK

First published in 1923 by Methuen & Co. Ltd

This edition first published in 2024
by Routledge
4 Park Square, Milton Park, Abingdon, Oxon OX14 4RN

and by Routledge
605 Third Avenue, New York, NY 10158

Routledge is an imprint of the Taylor & Francis Group, an informa business

© 1923 Methuen & Co. Ltd.

British Library Cataloguing in Publication Data
A catalogue record for this book is available from the British Library

ISBN: 978-1-032-80236-7 (Set)
ISBN: 978-1-032-82394-2 (Volume 17) (hbk)
ISBN: 978-1-032-82398-0 (Volume 17) (pbk)
ISBN: 978-1-003-50431-3 (Volume 17) (ebk)

DOI: 10.4324/9781003504313

Publisher's Note
The publisher has gone to great lengths to ensure the quality of this reprint but points out that some imperfections in the original copies may be apparent.

Disclaimer
The publisher has made every effort to trace copyright holders and would welcome correspondence from those they have been unable to trace.

THE FIXING OF WAGES
IN GOVERNMENT
EMPLOYMENT

BY

E. COLSTON SHEPHERD
B.A., B.Litt. (Oxon)

METHUEN & CO. LTD.
36 ESSEX STREET W.C.
LONDON

First Published in 1923

PRINTED IN GREAT BRITAIN

PREFACE

THE chief object of this study has been to collect and analyse the available material bearing on the Government practice in settling wages. This is done in the four chapters dealing with the War Office, Admiralty, Civil Service, and Post Office, which constitute the main substance of the work. In the introduction an attempt is made to indicate briefly the constitutional aspect of the problem and its relation to current economic theory on the subject of wages. The changes of the war period are summarized in Chapter V, though no attempt has been made to deal with these in such detailed fashion as the pre-war conditions are studied ; and the main conclusions are added.

CONTENTS

CHAPTER   PAGE

    PREFACE - - - - - - -   V

    INTRODUCTION -   -   -   -   -   xiii

Scope of Inquiry—Variety of occupations and size of wage-classes—Element of democratic control—Desire of Commons to secure " fair wages "—Bargaining inevitable—Yet Treasury control represents exercise of prerogative—No rigid definition of fair wages by Commons—Or acknowledged bases — Current economic theory — Necessary adaptation for present case—Demand and supply—No direct demand for Government products — How contact with a real demand is sought—Problems of the State.

I. THE WAR DEPARTMENT -   -   -   -   I

No scientific treatment of wages—Agitation the signal for revision—Pressure of high costs—Large factories and staffs but small peace-time production—Idle machinery and excessive supervision—The economy of inactivity—Overhead charges hold down wages—Mr. Haldane's admissions and recent War Office methods—Evidence of low wages—And of efficacy of industrial organization in raising them—Adoption by Department of Fair Wages Resolution—Put into effect only after pressure—Difficulty of applying " district rates "—The case of Farnborough—Piece-rates unsatisfactory—Speeding up—Fate of slow workers—Rate-cutting—Absence of guaranteed wage for piece-workers—Position of " skilled labourers "—The liability to re-classification with reduction of wages—Influence of the Treasury—Traditional advantages of Government workers—Non-existent for majority in War Department—Recent move of wages towards outside equivalent—Under pressure of trade union activities—Special problem of the Department remains unsolved—Leanings towards a distinctive wage-system have passed—Rejected by both sides.

CHAPTER   PAGE

II   THE ROYAL DOCKYARDS   -   -   -   -   27

Desire to isolate wage questions—Autocratic attitude of the Admiralty—Petitions but not negotiations — Wages are "prescribed" —And conditions "laid down" — This attitude has a beneficent aspect—Care for comfort of workers— Fair working of premium bonus system—Remoteness of the controlling power a disadvantage— Yard officers are often local arbiters—Admiralty's fear of change—Refusal to adopt "outside" rates— Parliamentary criticism — Unfavourable comparisons—The Fair Wages pledge—Difficulties in fulfilment—Because of special system of industrial organization—A minimum of change—Hence, "skilled labourers"—Their work and wages— Wages of similar labour outside—Justified on grounds of continuity of employment—Trade unionists' attack—Ineffective against Admiralty conservatism—Wages lower than those of private shipyards—The value of privileges—Tardy recognition of cost of living—Keen attention to economy —The charge of slackness on the part of workers— Small danger of dismissal for "established" workers—The case of the "hired" men is different —Effect of geographical isolation on wages—Good pay when necessary to "attract" workers—Trade union interference resented—Because it introduced alien principles—The evolution of wage peculiarities —Failure of a distinctive system—Through faults on both sides.

III.   THE CIVIL SERVICE   -   -   -   -   -   62

Unique nature of the employment—Recruiting and its aims—General ability for specialized work— Education the main test—Payment for educational qualifications—Effect of market rates on salaries— The Treasury's supply and demand test—Applied to women—Value of "privileges" forgotten in employment of "temporary" labour—Advantage taken of the monopolist position—Treasury veto on office requirements—High-grade work at lower pay—An economy ruse at the Post Office—Promotion uncommon and disadvantageous—Indistinct line between work of different grades— Speeding up—Grievance of low minima—Increase of "temporary" labour—With long service, low pay and no pensions—Saving expense—No relation of pay to effort—Particularly in case of women—

CONTENTS

CHAPTER   PAGE

Flat-rate overtime—Late acceptance of cost of living principle—Treasury's restricted outlook—Its view of the "model employer"—Collective bargaining opposed—Assistant clerks and a living wage—Attraction of the Service—Despite partial breakdown of "establishment" system—This popularity has been turned to account by Treasury—Humanitarian principles of secondary importance.

IV.   THE POST OFFICE -   -   -   -   -   89

A detached industry—Incapable of producing profit and loss account—Yet productive of large revenue—Ordinary business tests inapplicable—Real wage basis, demand and supply—Fluctuations in response to market conditions—Subordinate principles—Mass payment by results—Set up without due investigation—And without relation to changes in method of working—Payment for status rather than work—Individual service not assessed—The monopolist employer—Wage-schedules and cost of living—Comparative tables—Slow acknowledgment of real wages—The "living wage" ignored—Importance of current wages—Cheap labour—Low minima—The pay of pensioners—Speeding up—Departure from the "establishment" rule—Convenient and cheap—Poor pay of auxiliaries—The suspicion of sweating—Anomalous distinctions—Substitution duty and its remuneration—Overtime avoided by "split" duties—Or mostly paid for at flat rate—Female labour, admittedly cheap—Rural postmen and farm wages—These examples point the advantage taken by the Department of its monopolist position—Advantages of the "established" servants—Incremental scales obscure work values—The move towards special pay at the "age of responsibility"—Opposition offered by workers to the wage-system—Collective bargaining refused—The alternative, Parliamentary pressure—A remarkable agitation—Political threats—M.P.'s. intimidated—Postmaster-General coerced—The ludicrous and the dangerous aspects—Action justified by prohibition of other methods—The danger non-recurrent—The arbitrament of Select Committees—Steady pressure of workers—A large degree of standardization conceded—Fundamental conceptions of wages unchanged—Inordinate attraction of the Service—Summary and conclusions.

CHAPTER   PAGE
V.   RECENT DEVELOPMENTS   -   -   -   -   129

    War-time expansion—New needs and new
methods—Maintenance of real wages—Arbitration
machinery—Fresh problems raised by manual
labour were transitory—Insistence of disparity
between wages of men and of women—The case
of permanent Government workers—Civil Service
Arbitration Board—Effect of cost of living on high
salaries—Graded bonuses—The underlying principles—"Additional responsibilities" acknowledged
—Women's increases—Basic rates practically unaltered—War-time negotiations opened way to
collective bargaining—This had become a necessity
to the Departments—Hence, Whitley Councils—
Adopted for *industrial* establishments after some
misgivings—And under safeguards—Craft divisions
accentuated—New attitude of Treasury—Veto
modified—Closer touch with workers—Work of
Joint Industrial Councils—Trade unions refused to
be ousted—Failure of Admiralty's attempt—
Non-manual classes not included in these schemes—
A poor imitation offered—And rejected—A joint
plan substituted—Willing definition of limitations—
Smooth working—Government repents—Arbitration Board abolished—Treasury resumes veto—
Retrogression—General effect of Whitley Councils
—Significance of the change—Greater industrial
security.

VI.   THE METHODS OF FOREIGN GOVERNMENTS   -   152

    Reflect stage of political development—Character-
istics common to all—Automatic wage-progression
weakening—Australia and the "living wage"—
An example not largely followed—European ban
on full collective bargaining—France, Holland,
Germany, Austria—The wages of women—The
influence of the "living wage" in this—Wage fixing
not scientifically dealt with—Adjustment brought
about only by pressure—Instance of the United
States of America—Remarkable fall in real wages
since 1893—Except where Government was not a
monopolistic employer—Competition and agitation
—The only effective weapon against inertia—The
effect of "outside" rates—Lack of wage policy,
has meant adoption of commercial standards.

PAGE

CONCLUSIONS - - - - - - 163

Demand and supply dominant—Weakening of
the modifying influences—The older ideals—And
their partial abandonment—Why " commercial "
standards crept in—The Treasury indicted—
Treasury and House of Commons both misunderstood spirit of original system—And sought to
remove its distinctiveness—The interpretation of
the Departments—What the ideal meant—Advent
of collective bargaining has helped—Was the change
inevitable ?—Security and high endeavour—The
constitutional aspect of the change—Possible effect
politically, of recent experience—Problem of
providing incentive to effort, is unsolved—Yet
moral principles are looked for in Government
employment.

APPENDIX A - - - - - - 172

APPENDIX B - - - - - - 194

APPENDIX C - - - - - - 196

INDEX - - - - - - - 203

INTRODUCTION

A STUDY of the methods and systems by which wages are fixed for Government employees brings under notice a large range of occupations. Some of these are peculiar to Government employment, some are common to industry in general, but in respect to all of them—from the highly paid permanent secretary of a Government department to the unskilled labourer in a Royal dockyard or national factory—payments are made in return for work done or services rendered. Such payments and the modes of arriving at them are the subject of the present inquiry. The variety of wage questions is therefore large, for the dockyards of the Admiralty alone employ a host of different craftsmen and professional workers. The Post Office too has many different grades, chiefly of a specialized type. In all departments there are classes of workers whose wages involve varying treatment and special consideration. Not only is the question of interest in point of variety : it is also of importance since it covers so large a body of wage-earners.

The Post Office, in 1914, had in its employment 240,000 workers,[1] and the Civil Service at the same time numbered about 60,000.[2] The War Office, at the beginning of 1922, when it had practically

[1] Fourth Report, Royal Commission on Civil Service (Cd. 7338 of 1914), par. 4.
[2] *Ibid.*, par. 5.

recovered from the extraordinary conditions of the war, employed about 45,000 persons. The numbers on the books of the Admiralty between 1900 and 1906 varied between 27,000 and 35,000.[1] In later years the number was much nearer 50,000. The Office of Works finds employment for about 5,000, and the Air Ministry at the end of 1921 employed at least 10,000 wage-earners. At least 400,000 workers are concerned therefore, and it is probable that at present the number of persons receiving wages from the Government is not far short of half a million.

Special interest attaches to this study, however, because the wage systems are ultimately the product of democratic control. The House of Commons has the first and last word in the matter of national finance. The Commons vote the sums of money required ; Parliament enacts that certain sums be granted to the Crown for specific purposes ; under that authority the Treasury issues money ; the Auditor-General checks and audits ; and finally the Commons receive a report as to the expenditure. Subject to the subsequent approval of Parliament, the Treasury has a good deal of discretionary power ; yet if it is remembered that the Treasury is very closely associated with the Cabinet as a whole, that the Prime Minister is usually First Lord, and that the Chancellor of the Exchequer is practically a Treasury official, the Finance Department may be assumed to carry out usually the policy of a Cabinet which reflects the views of the Commons. Since the Commons are democratically elected, their policy must be at least acquiesced in by the community. Thus it may be reasonably expected that the wage

[1] " Hansard," July 9, 1906 : Statement by Mr. Edmund Robertson.

bargain in Government employment shall be fair and shall not seek to take advantage of any of the disabilities from which the workers suffer. The will of the House of Commons to be fair is seen in the terms which the Fair Wages Clause in Government contracts imposes on contractors.[1] The word " bargain," however, is an awkward term, though really more objectionable in appearance than in fact. It has seemed inappropriate that a sovereign body should have to strike a bargain with its workers. To a Department like the Admiralty it has been almost repugnant. Actually, in the industrial sphere of national affairs, it imposes no greater limitation on sovereignty than is imposed, in the ordinary constitutional sphere, by the " general will." Dicey has pointed out that alongside the *legal* fact that Parliament

---

[1] The first Fair Wages Resolution was carried by the House of Commons in 1891. The new resolution, carried on March 10, 1909, was as follows : " The contractor shall, under a penalty of a fine or otherwise, pay rates of wages and observe hours of labour not less favourable than those commonly recognized by employers and trade societies (or, in the absence of such recognized wages and hours, those which in practice prevail amongst good employers) in the trade in the district where the work is carried out. Where there are no such hours recognized or prevailing in the district, those recognized or prevailing in the nearest district in which the general industrial circumstances are similar shall be adopted. Further, the conditions of employment generally accepted in the district in the trade concerned shall be taken into account in considering how far the terms of the Fair Wage Clauses are being observed. The contractor shall be prohibited from transferring or assigning, directly or indirectly, to any person or persons whatever, any portion of his contract without the written permission of the department. Sub-letting other than that which may be customary in the trade concerned shall be prohibited. The contractor shall be responsible for the observance of the Fair Wages Clauses by the sub-contractor." —" Hansard."

is the sovereign power must be set the *practical* limitation on that sovereignty, which exists in " the possibility or certainty that the subjects or a large part of them will resist or disobey the sovereign laws. "[1] In this is implied a sort of civic bargain, from which the industrial bargain is not irreconcilably different. Our national disinclination to admit facts in blunt terms has retarded an acknowledgment of this. The bargain, even the collective bargain, has existed, for the failure of the Admiralty to attract engineering artisans until they offered higher wages[2] meant that the workers as a whole had rejected the terms originally offered and demanded certain others, which were eventually conceded. The idea of bargaining, except of the individual type, in which each worker accepted or rejected prescribed terms, was but slowly admitted in national establishments.

Apart from the Fair Wages Resolutions the House of Commons has not approached wage questions very closely or attempted to regulate in detail the wages paid to those workers whom the State employed direct. The Treasury has held the reins in this matter. Under its supervision, employing Departments have prescribed rates of wages. The Postmaster-General (Mr. H. C. Raikes) in 1891 submitted a long and persuasive letter to the Treasury, asking for approval of new rates for postmen.[3] To all Departments the Treasury has given a certain licence, an instance of which may be found in a minute which

[1] Dicey : " Law of the Constitution," Part I, Chap. I, p. 74 (8th edition).
[2] See pp. 31 and 59.
[3] Unpublished Report of the Raikes Inquiry into the Post Office. See Appendix C.

still governs the action of the Office of Works. This minute declares that the First Commissioner of Works may " fix rates paid to men direct, provided that the proposed changes do not affect whole classes of employees, do not depend upon considerations of policy, and are not such as to give rise to claims in other public Departments."[1] Wages have evidently been looked upon as administrative matters. In effect, wage questions have been treated very largely as a matter of prerogative ; yet this does not alter the fact of democratic control, for, as Dicey points out, the prerogative is really exercised by Ministers, and Ministers are really the servants *not* of the Crown but of a representative chamber, which, in turn, obeys the behests of the electors.[2]

The ultimate authority therefore is the electorate, and the view taken by that electorate as to some of the peculiarities of labour may be gauged by its legislation. From the repeal of the Combination Acts in 1824-5 there have been many industrial enactments, of which may be mentioned the Factory Acts, the Mines Regulations Acts of 1843 and 1860, the Nine Hours Act for the cotton workers in 1875, and the Trades Union Acts of 1871 and 1913. There is no actual wage legislation amongst these, but it is significant that trade unions were legalized sooner in this country than in any other, and there is ample recognition of the need for collective bargaining or an equivalent safeguard.

Enactment as to wages has never taken the form of direct fixing of wages by Parliament or a central

---

[1] Communicated orally by official of the Office of Works.
[2] Dicey : " Law of the Constitution," Part III, Chap. XV, p. 463 (8th edition).

Government Department, except during the war. Legislation, like the Trade Boards Acts, has touched only the fringe of the problem. The subject is peculiarly difficult, because there is no accepted fundamental basis upon which to estimate wages.[1]

The study of economics has sought to explain the general principles on which, as a matter of fact, wages are settled, but this theory merely summarizes what determines wages in ordinary enterprise, without attempting to offer guidance to a legislator or administrator who is compelled by the circumstances of his position to interfere with wages. The ordinary economic theory requires some modification, for though the product of a Government Department is supplied according to the same considerations of utility as an ordinary commodity, it is not supplied in the open market, and in most cases wages cannot depend upon the demand for the product.

Hence a government cannot apply the ordinary tests suggested by the theory of wages to the pay of its workers. In some instances it may be possible for a Government Department to work out rent and profits. Generally such a statement cannot be produced, and in the most favourable of cases it would be misleading. The Post Office, which comes nearest to supplying services for which there is an expressed demand, is a monopolist concern, and therefore does not sell its product (or services) under ordinary market conditions. Further, it is primarily a service and performs some functions for which no payment is

[1] Webb: "Industrial Democracy," Chap. IV, p. 229 (1920 Ed.).

made.[1] The conditions of supply of the product have made the fixing of wages in Government employment a difficult question. The desire to establish contact with an expressed demand for the product is reflected in the terms of the Fair Wages Resolution.[2] " District rates " were adopted wherever it was possible to apply them. For fixing wages in the Civil Service and the Post Office no such device was available, and the relation of wages in those Departments to a real demand could never be more than roughly achieved. Nevertheless, a loose contact with the wages of private enterprise is established, since theoretically a Government must compete with other employers for the labour it needs.[3] This is a substitute for the market demand which influences wages in ordinary enterprise. And it is the only method by which a Government may measure the output it receives in return for the wages paid. Hence it may be said that, in fact, private enterprise will regulate the rates of wages in a Government undertaking.

In practice, this has been occasionally taken to mean that the adequacy of wages in Government employment may be tested by the supply of labour which is attracted. This, however, ignores the influence exerted by the prospects of security and continuity of employment upon those who have labour to sell. Nevertheless, it is stated to have been a rule of the Treasury not to sanction increases of wage-

[1] See p. 89.
[2] *Supra*, p. xv.
[3] This is implied in the conclusion arrived at by the Royal Commission on the Civil Service, 1914, that prospects offered to candidates for the first division should be " equally eligible " with those of other professions.

rates unless it was shown that labour would not be forthcoming at the old price. [1]

Thus the State has had to meet three large problems in dealing with wages. First, it has sought to arrive at wages that are economically sound—wages which are a true reflex of supply and demand, despite the fact that the services rendered can have no expressed market value. Secondly, there has rested upon the State an obligation to avoid taking advantage of the weaknesses of the workers. This was clearly a moral necessity, since collective bargaining was not acknowledged until quite recently. Finally, the State has been set the problem of resolving the apparent incompatibility of the collective bargain with sovereignty.

Wage conditions in the various Departments are here examined, with these points in view. Distinctive features are to be found in the wage systems of all Departments. These are analysed, and the value of devices not generally found in private employment is estimated in the light of available evidence.

---

[1] *Infra,* p. 67.

THE FIXING OF WAGES IN GOVERNMENT EMPLOYMENT

CHAPTER I

THE WAR DEPARTMENT

PRIOR to the formal acceptance by the War Office in 1912 of the spirit of the Fair Wages Resolution, the Department's method of dealing with the wages of such workers as it employed direct was one which involved perhaps the least trouble and produced the least uniform results. Conditions of employment had grown up without any very serious attempt to base them upon a defensible principle. Rates of wages had been arrived at by various processes. Their adjustment had taken place, if at all, in response to labour pressure. No definite standard was set, and wages seem to have depended very largely upon what the workers would accept, advantage being taken of the privileges which Government workers enjoyed, though even these were not scientifically assessed until 1911. Improvements in rates were decided by a variety of influences, but the moving force always was the demand of the workers themselves. Thus, an instruction for " civilian subordinates " issued in 1904 says : " Petitions from civilian subordinates for increased wages will not be forwarded to the War

Office, but the officer in charge of the Department will submit, through the general officer commanding, such recommendations regarding the approved rates of wages as he may find to be necessary." [1]   These recommendations were the signal for investigations ; they were the inception of revisions.   Where possible comparison was made with outside rates, and to a certain extent such rates were accepted as a guide, though in the past they were not adopted with the same precision as now, because incremental systems were preferred.

Actually, War Office wages were generally below those paid for similar work by private employers. The discrepancy varied with different grades from 2s. to 4s. per week,[2] and at Woolwich, where a great deal of piecework was done, keen criticism was made of the fixing of prices.   It is evident that the War Office in these matters was subject to pressure not less severe than that of competition on private employers. Much of the work for which the Arsenal and War Department factories are fitted has always been done by contractors, and the test by which the production of these establishments has been judged is cost, as compared with the prices at which contractors offer to do similar work.   Also the War Office has for years

[1] War Office Regulations for Civilian Subordinates (1904), Sec. V, par. 33.   The corresponding provision in the amended Regulations issued in 1922 (Sec. I, par. 14) states : " A petition from a class or group of employees must, in the first instance, be submitted to the local head of the department. If it cannot be acceded to locally, it will be forwarded to the War Office by the general officer commanding, with such observations as he may desire to make. . . ."

[2] Pamphlet issued by United Government Workers' Federation (December, 1910) : " Case for Increase in the Minimum Wage for Enfield and Waltham." Also oral statement by Mr. Jack Mills (A.E.U.)

sought to obtain contracts for arms and munitions required by other Government Departments, chiefly the Admiralty. Here again price was an important— sometimes the most important—item. To complicate this matter there has been another difficulty. Parliament has desired that the national factories should be maintained in such a condition that their productive capacity could be rapidly expanded in case of war. It has never, however, offered any solution of the problem as to how this could be done without making the peace-time activity of these factories either excessive or unduly expensive. This is a dilemma which the War Office has still to solve. An establishment like Woolwich Arsenal has always a large proportion of its machinery standing idle in peace-time, and has usually a skeleton personnel, in the form of superintendents, foremen, shop managers, etc., far in excess of the staff actually required for the work in hand. Throughout the present century the problem has handicapped the War Office and impeded the workers in their efforts to improve wages. The depreciation of idle machinery has to be provided for out of current account ; the pay of superfluous supervisors has to be charged to the cost of production ; yet, nevertheless, tenders for contracts must compare favourably with the terms which private firms offer. Instances of the difficulties created are readily available. In July, 1907, the Henderson Committee reported : " We learn that 43 per cent. of the machinery in the Royal Carriage Department, Royal Gun Factory (exclusive of the Torpedo Factory), and Royal Laboratory was idle in the week ended March 2, 1907." [1] In the same year

[1] Henderson Committee on Production of Marketable Articles at Woolwich Arsenal (Cd. 3514 of 1907), par. 15.

it was stated that one contract for nearly £8,000 was lost to the Arsenal simply because an indirect charge of over £2,000 had to be added to the actual cost of production in respect of establishment maintenance.[1] This is probably a fair indication of the type of difficulty which the War Office has met in the matter of arranging its wages, and since this amounts to an addition of at least 20 per cent. to the cost of production, is not surprising if wages for some years were below the market rate and if piecework prices were cut to a very fine point.

As to the maintaining of a large supervising staff, an interesting example is provided by the following extract, which refers to the condition of the Arsenal in March, 1909—a time when no danger of war had arisen for some years, and when the manual workers employed were at a very low figure :—

" It is a remarkable fact that at a time when the strength of the [Royal Gun] factory is down to the unprecedented minimum of 1,500, the staff of the factory is the same, with the exception of a rearrangement of the duties of a few assistant foremen, as when 5,000 men were fully employed. Omitting all consideration of the clerical staff, estimate clerks, worktakers, viewers, warders, gaugers, and leading hands, and the proportion of the cost of upkeep of the Central Office, the supervising staff consists at the present moment of the following :

[1] " Hansard," March 11, 1908. Mr. Will Crooks said : " Recently the Royal Carriage Department was asked for an estimate for the manufacture of stores. The estimated price worked out at £9,633 12s. as against £7,964, the trade price. . . . An analysis of the price was submitted to the Army Council. . . . The analysis proved that of the £9,633 12s. no less a sum than £2,417 1s. was charged as general indirect expenditure."

Assistant Superintendent	-	-	I
Manager	-	-	-	-	I
Assistant Managers	-	-	-	3
Shop Managers	-	-	-	-	3
Supervisor	-	-	-	-	-	I
Foremen and Assistant Foremen	-	45

Total   -   -   54

Allowing for part services of the Superintendent, who is also in charge of the Royal Carriage Department, this works out at one official for every 27 men." [1]

It has never been an easy matter for the War Department to decide to keep its factories working at anything like full speed in peace time, but the spirit of economy, as embodied in a non-productive policy, has been most accentuated since the conclusion of the South African War. From 1897–9 the workers in the Arsenal numbered from 13,500 to 13,700, but by 1908 the strength was only from 8,000 to 8,400. [2] It was the workers naturally who pressed at this time for the idle machinery to be employed and for more hands to be given work. They urged, in deputation

[1] " Woolwich Pioneer," March 12, 1909. The above proportion may be compared with corresponding figures for the Royal Dockyards in the same year, which showed a proportion of one official for every 65 men.
" Hansard," July 5, 1909 : " Mr. McKenna said the number at present borne (exclusive of the Works Department) was :

Principal Officers	 II
Superior Officers	 41
Subordinate Officers	 40
Inspectors	 67
Workmen ..	.. .. .. 10,441 "

[2] Letter from Woolwich and District Trades and Labour Council to Prime Minister, published in " Woolwich Pioneer," April 17, 1908.

and through members of Parliament, that horseshoes for the Army might be made in the Arsenal, and that agricultural implements might be manufactured. Strangely enough, it was the former suggestion, which involved but little use of machinery, and necessitated some expenditure in plant, that was accepted, though not until the tenders had been found able to bear comparison with outside costs. "I understand," wrote a newspaper contributor in March, 1908, "that the estimates submitted by the Ordnance Factories, subject to sufficient orders being placed to meet the initial cost of plant, are so satisfactory that it is almost a certainty that an order will be placed with the factories of at least 4,000 pairs of shoes per week." [1]

The necessity to meet competition in this way, despite the burden of a war-time establishment, was a serious stumbling-block through the first decade of this century. Mr. Haldane, during his term as Secretary of State for War, admitted it frankly,[2] and advanced it without scruple as an indisputable reason why War Office wages could not rise to the level of those in outside employment. To a deputation in February, 1911, this excuse was put forward by him.

---

[1] "Woolwich Pioneer," March 20, 1908.
[2] *Ibid.*, October 23, 1908. Mr. Haldane, speaking at the dinner of the Royal Arsenal Association of Foremen, was reported thus : " By the constitution of the Army and Navy and the financial departments of the country, you have at once to produce the equipments of the Army at something like reasonable prices, and to include in that price the cost of maintaining a reserve power for war. No other business has that problem. I wish it were differently shaped, because I feel it is a problem that can never be solved satisfactorily. Departments ask : ' Why don't you give us the things we want at the same price that we pay elsewhere, and we should send you a great deal of work ? ' "

" If I can get things cheaper from the contractor, I must go to the contractor for them," he replied to their plea for higher wages, and in the next breath came this admission : " We keep up Woolwich to a war footing only because we are not extravagant." [1] Again in the following year the story was the same. In February, 1912, Mr. Haldane again told a wages deputation : " We produce for other Departments as well as for ourselves, and we are bound to produce at not very much more cost than the private firms or the Departments will go to the contractors." [2]

It is clear that the War Office, to-day, would not admit that these conditions held down wages, or even that the overhead charges are excessive in comparison with private employment. It has been suggested that they are simply equivalent to " such outgoings as advertising, dividends, interests on loans, and insurance," which a private firm has to take into account. The comparison does not hold good to any great degree, for in private industry, most of these items are variable in response to trade fluctuations, while the Arsenal charge is definitely fixed.[3]

[1] Eighth Quarterly Report of Parliamentary Committee, Trades Union Congress, March, 1911.

[2] Eleventh Quarterly Report of Parliamentary Committee, Trades Union Congress, March, 1912.

[3] Since wages came more or less into line with those of private employment, the plea of heavy oncost has been dropped, and the policy of dealing with the workers entirely reversed. It is now held that overhead charges are not excessive, but that production is costly because of slackness on the part of the workers. The following is an extract from the Minutes of the Engineering Trade Joint Council for Government Departments, Tenth Meeting, January 4, 1922, (circulated to representatives) : " Mr. —— outlined in some detail the considerations which had forced upon him the conviction that the men in Woolwich were not giving as

Thus handicapped, the War Office was extremely unwilling to move in the matter of wages. A steady and continuous pressure was applied, however, by the workers, particularly by the Woolwich contingent, and in a less degree by the men at Enfield and Waltham and the clothing operatives at Pimlico. From 1908 an agitation for a minimum of 30s. a week was carried on. The wages of all Government labourers in the London district had been raised in 1906 from 21s. to 23s. At the latter figure they remained until the outbreak of war. At the same time the skilled workers kept up a demand for trade union rates. The carpenters and joiners in 1907 put forward their claim for the trade union rate for London of 10½d. an hour instead of the existing rates of 8d. to 10d. paid at the Arsenal.[1] Workers at the Pimlico Clothing Factory enlisted the support of Mr. Ramsay Macdonald and the Labour members for the application of Parliamentary pressure. They held up as examples of low wages the facts that of 480 storehouse men and porters employed at Pimlico in 1910, 440 were receiving 23s. per week and the remainder 25s. ; that skilled tailoresses on piecework averaged only 17s. 5½d. per week, though in private employment they would earn from 30s. to 35s. ; and that as piece-rates were

much for the £1, as comparable men outside. . . . He could prove beyond dispute that the oncost chargeable against labour at Woolwich was less than the oncost at a comparable concern. This fact must be accepted. Consequently the excessive cost of output meant either that the administration at Woolwich was faulty, or the same effort was not being put forth by the men. Woolwich could not even compete in the manufacture of articles like fuses, for which it was specially adapted."

[1] " Woolwich Pioneer," August 23, 1907. Report of Deputation to Mr. F. D. Acland.

computed on time-rates, especially competent women whose piece-earnings exceeded the basic time-wage, had had their wages reduced.[1] The Government Workers' Federation, on behalf of workers at Enfield and Waltham, carried out in 1910 a local survey which they submitted to the War Office, showing that the rate paid by the Department to its unskilled workers in those factories was not only 3s. a week less than the average for such labour in the district, but was actually 3s. 3d. per week less than that paid by the contractor employing labourers on work in the Royal Small Arms Factory itself. They showed, too, that labourers working in the danger building at Waltham were still receiving 23s. 6d., a wage which had remained unaltered since 1894.[2] In one case only had real success attended the efforts of the workers up to 1910. The engineers, splendidly organized and acting unitedly did in 1908 obtain an increase in their wages from 37s. to 40s. per week, with a reduction of 1s. 6d. for men working at the Arsenal " in consideration of emoluments."[3] Mr. F. D. Acland himself admitted that the solidarity of the engineers had been responsible for this success, and practically advised other grades to present united demands in similar fashion if they would succeed.[4] Combination, however, was of slow

[1] "Hansard," March 7, 1910.

[2] Pamphlet issued by the Government Workers' Federation (December, 1910) : " Case for an Increase in the Minimum Wage for Enfield and Waltham."

[3] " Woolwich Pioneer," November 13, 1908. Report of Deputation from Labour Protection League to Mr. F. D. Acland.

[4] *Ibid.* Mr. Acland is reported thus : " The men if they desired to succeed in their efforts must drop sectional representation. They must unite in a body not alone in the Arsenal but throughout the country, and then the Government would not be able to withstand their appeal."

growth in the face of discouragement, avowed and implied. An instance of this came before the House of Commons in 1910 when Mr. Bowerman raised the question as to an Army Order of 1908 " ordaining that the men employed at Weedon must cease to belong to the Army Ordnance Departments Employees' Union." The reply of Mr. Haldane that this applied only to pensionable employees, i.e. foremen, rendered the fiat less objectionable, but it is evident that it had been assumed by the workers to apply to all grades.[1]   While the pressure from the labour side was not overwhelming, the War Office stood firmly by its old wage bases.   One reply to the demand for a 30s. minimum at Woolwich took the form of statistics prepared by the Board of Trade to show that while there had been a rise in the cost of commodities between 1905 and 1908 of from 4 to 5 per cent., there had been a reduction in rent of about 9 per cent., and on these grounds the minimum of 23s. could not be increased.[2]

In 1910 the terms of the Fair Wages Resolution, passed by the House of Commons the preceding year, were accepted by the War Office for application to the workers it employed direct.[3]   It was assumed that henceforth rates " not less favourable than those recognized by employers and trade societies in the

[1] " Hansard," April 5, 1910.
[2] " Woolwich Pioneer," November 13, 1908. Report of Deputation from Labour Protection League to Mr. F. D. Acland.
[3] " Hansard," March 8, 1910. In the debate on Mr. R. Macdonald's Fair Wages Resolution, Mr. Sydney Buxton (President of the Board of Trade) said : " In consequence of the acceptance by the House of Commons last March of a resolution which I moved, considerably extending and defining the Fair Wages Clause, we have instituted, and it is working most satisfactorily, a committee on which the various spending

district "[1] would be granted to all workers. In the following year, however, pressure was still being applied to bring this about. The Trades Union Congress passed a resolution demanding " trade union rates of wages " for all Government workers, and a deputation from the Parliamentary Committee urged the matter before the War Minister, Mr. Haldane, in February, 1911.[2] The awkward point in these negotiations was to arrive at agreement as to the money value of the privileges which War Office workmen enjoyed. In this, as in the matter of adjusting wages, the War Office moved reluctantly, and again only under the stimulus of external occurrences. The National Health Insurance Act of 1911 provided the necessary pressure, for it rendered superfluous one of the " privileges " and led to an examination of all the extras—sick pay, medical attendance, public holidays, and gratuity on discharge. These were at last subjected to an assessment, and an approximate value of 1s. per £ of wages set upon them. Sick pay and medical attendance were the chief concern. These were separately estimated as worth 6d. in the pound, were removed from the list of privileges, and the workers as a whole

departments are represented, under the chairmanship of Mr. Askwith of the Board of Trade. . . .

" The suggestion I make on behalf of my right honourable friend is that, if complaint is made that wages directly paid by the War Office at Pimlico, Weedon, or elsewhere are not what they ought to be in comparison with the wages paid outside, he is prepared to refer the matter to this committee, and to take their advice into consideration with a view to placing matters on a satisfactory basis."

[1] " Hansard," March 10, 1909 : Fair Wages Resolution,

[2] Eighth Quarterly Report, Parliamentary Committee, March, 1911.

were compensated by an increase in their wages at the rate of 6d. in the pound. A similar value therefore was assumed to be set upon the remaining items, but still movement towards the application of the Fair Wages Resolution was slow, and in February, 1912, the Parliamentary Committee of the Trades Union Congress was again assailing the Secretary of State for War on wages questions, and urging him to post in all workshops of the Department a notice as to the acceptance of " district rates." [1] Subsequently the notice demanded was issued and posted, and in theory at all events the principle was established and publicly announced. The notice, in poster form, left little doubt as to the intention of the Department, for it incorporated the vital phrases from the Fair Wages Resolution itself : " The wages and hours of labour of workmen employed by the War Department are regulated in accordance with the Resolution passed by the House of Commons on the 10th March, 1909, relating to Government contracts ; that is, the Government will pay rates of wages and observe hours of labour not less favourable than those commonly recognized by employers and trade societies (or, in the absence of such recognized wages and hours, those which in practice prevail amongst good employers) in the trade in the district where the work is carried out. Where there are no such wages and hours recognized or prevailing in the district, those recognized or prevailing in the nearest district in which the general industrial circumstances are similar, shall be adopted.—By Order." [2]

[1] Eleventh Quarterly Report, Parliamentary Committee of Trades Union Congress, March, 1912.
[2] Poster G 12/200, issued by War Office, 1912.

" District rates " have never been an easy subject. The production of the War Department in its various factories frequently has no parallel in the same district. Some of its establishments have been put down in neighbourhoods which were otherwise purely agricultural, and the effect has been to change a whole series of conditions. In fact, the establishment of a War Office factory has made a set of conditions of which the district, in its old and geographical sense, could offer no interpretation. An influx of industrialists in a thinly populated district drove the cost of house-room to a prohibitive figure, caused the price of commodities to rise, and gave the workers a sense of victimization which only a generous wage allowance could have mollified. The War Office had no machinery for grappling with a situation of this sort. Accustomed to move slowly and always along well-defined and acknowledged lines, it yielded on such points only after very determined pressure. The Royal Aircraft Factory at Farnborough is an instance of such an upheaval. It grew from a small balloon depot, and by the beginning of 1913 was expanding rapidly and providing work for a large and increasing body of men, skilled and unskilled. For most of the crafts concerned there was no analogy in the district. A few labourers, storekeepers, and building workers retained at Aldershot formed some sort of basis, but no real comparison, because of the artificial state of affairs which the mushroom growth of population at Farnborough created. Unskilled labourers at this factory received from 20s. to 22s. a week (1s. to 3s. less than the equivalent grade at Woolwich), while operative engineers and craftsmen generally were paid 2s. 6d. per week less than similar workers in the

Arsenal.[1]   Members of the A.S.E. in June, 1913, took the matter seriously in hand.   They had already talked and written to the War Office on the subject without result.   Now a joint committee was formed to arrange a plan of action which should " compel officialism to see " that Government employees were " determined to obtain a living wage." [2]   The agitation of this body (strengthened by the outbreak of war in 1914) succeeded after slightly more than a year, and in August, 1914, the rates were raised almost to the level of the Arsenal workers, and the Department was turning its attention to the housing question.[3] To-day skilled men at Farnborough receive the London rate plus a small addition in consequence of the care and precision which the work demands.

Thus even for time rates of wages the " district " rule has not always proved an absolutely reliable test. Piecework rates throughout have been a source of grievance to the men.   At present the Department adopts as its standard in price-fixing the trade union rule that an average worker shall be able on piecework to earn time and a third, but this has come by a long path of criticism and complaint about the " feed and speed " and premium bonus systems, and about the absence of a guaranteed minimum time rate.   At Woolwich in 1907 a deputation from the Royal Carriage Department, complaining to the Chief Superintendent of Ordnance Factories, said " it was possible and had indeed happened for men to be at work and at the

[1] " A.S.E. Journal," October, 1914 : Report of Organizing Delegate, No. 9 District.
[2] Ibid., June, 1913 : Report of Organizing Delegate, No. 9 District.
[3] Ibid,, September, 1914 : Report of Organizing Delegate, No. 9 District.

end of the week only to be able to take a few shillings for the week's wages."[1] This statement was not challenged by the official side, nor was any hope of a rearrangement held out, and there was certainly some ground for the bitter remark of the journal reporting this meeting that " Government factories expect men to spend 48 hours in a shop on the off-chance of a piecework job."[2] In 1911 the Trades Union Congress was appealing to the Secretary of State for War to discontinue piecework in the danger buildings at Woolwich on the ground that it caused hurry and therefore danger to the lives of the workers. On the wages side of the question the Congress had an equally serious indictment to bring. It protested against the system of " feed and speed " which, in the words of the resolution, " harasses the workman, reduces his earnings, and generally creates conditions akin to sweating."[3] The deputies who laid the case before Mr. Haldane claimed that it not only unfairly reduced wages but also that accidents, since the introduction of the system, had increased by 50 per cent.[4] The War Minister's defence was the old economy cry, but some of his admissions were interesting: " We have been making a very thorough investigation " ; " We have dealt with a great many cases " ; " In all the cases we have gone into we have revised the system."[5] Revision on such a scale seems to prove that the allegations of the men were not wholly without foundation. Wages evidently had suffered under the new

[1] Woolwich Pioneer," July 12, 1907.
[2] *Ibid.*
[3] Eighth Quarterly Report, Parliamentary Committee, Trades Union Congress, March, 1911.
[4] *Ibid.*
[5] *Ibid.*

piecework system. Something, too, of the heavier demands upon the men is seen in the increase of accidents, but the most striking proof of the incidence of the new system may be gathered from the fate of some of the older workers. On this subject the following paragraph may be quoted : " Between the 1st June, 1906, and the 1st June, 1907, the startling number of 869 men with ten years' service and over were discharged from the Arsenal. . . . One shop manager in the West Laboratory, momentarily breaking through the usual official reserve, let out the brutal truth when in answer to a long-service man's query for the reason for his discharge, [he] replied that ' he was too old for the job.' Yet this man was under forty years of age." [1]

Rate-fixing and rate-cutting appear to have become synonymous terms under this system. This was partly due no doubt to the need for a defensive policy in view of the increasing pressure from the labour side, and of the unwillingness of the men to have a piece price reduced if it was found to have been fixed too high. Formerly a generous price was set for a new job, and when the wage sheets were examined adjustment downwards was often made. The letter of a rate fixer dealing with the changed methods is illuminating. " The old-fashioned method," he wrote in 1908, " was to put on a good big price, then when a large number had been made down came the price and down-grade prices were general. Our methods are entirely different. We work the prices out from a scientific basis, starting the job at a low figure, then we can add on if required, and sometimes double the original price when neces-

---

[1] " Woolwich Pioneer," June 21, 1909.

sary." [1] Such methods of course amounted to rate cutting for the moment, even though no price had previously been in existence for the particular job. Mr. Haldane was continually approached on the subject, and he appears to have given a ruling in 1911 (which, while valuable to the men, did not touch the root of this trouble) that there should be no reduction of piecework prices " unless new and improved methods or tools are introduced." [2] Still the trouble remained. Men even in the danger buildings often found their wages on piecework for a full week to be considerably below the time rate to which their craft entitled them. The following newspaper paragraph of April 18, 1913, gives one example : " The discontent which has been smouldering for so long in the danger buildings against the conditions of employment came to a head on Friday last in the Cannon Cartridge Factory, where the men received their pay tickets with 10s. to 15s.

[1] "Woolwich Pioneer," October 9, 1908.

[2] *Ibid.*, May 31, 1912. It was not until 1915 that this principle was embodied in an official notice to the workers. The following is a copy of an announcement issued in August, 1915 :—

" PIECEWORK EARNINGS.

" In order to remove any misapprehension which may exist, it is notified that no reductions are made in ' rate fixed ' piecework prices unless changes are made in the method of production. When that takes place the prices are fixed having regard to such changes of method.

" This, of course, does not apply to temporary or ' job ' prices.

" The above has been the unaltered practice before the war, and will be so continued both during and after the war without regard being paid to any special efforts which may now be made to expedite output.

" No limitation has been or will be imposed on the earnings of piece-workers.

" *7th August,* 1915.   (Sgd.) H. F. DONALDSON,
     " Chief Superintendent of Ordnance Factories."

2

deducted. For some time it seemed that the price-cutters had gone just the inch too far, and it was not until a deputation had received a promise of a full inquiry that work was resumed after dinner." [1] Another extract from the same newspaper shows that for the week ended June 15, 1913, pieceworkers in the danger buildings at Woolwich received 12s. 3d. each less than the time wages for such grades. [2]

It would perhaps be a fair answer to such citations to claim that they represent merely the process of arriving at a proper price, that few estimates can be absolutely accurate without experiment, and that such experiments are embodied in the cases quoted. It is clear, however, that the War Office intention was to keep rates down to the lowest point which the workers would accept. Two reasons for this may be advanced. Either the object was to stimulate pro-duction—a proceeding which is frequently necessary in Government employment—or the aim was to reduce to the minimum the cost of production per unit. When piecework conditions are examined alongside the treatment, during the same period, of time workers, appearances suggest that economy was the primary influence. It is significant too that the grades whose wages suffered most were those whose economic position and degree of organization were least strong. The War Office, following the lead of the Admiralty, has for long employed as a large percentage of its workers " skilled labourers " who owe such skill as they possess to their training in Government workshops and who, theoretically, are transferable when skilled work is short to the work and pay of ordinary

[1] " Woolwich Pioneer," April 18, 1913.
[2] *Ibid.*, June 20, 1913.

labourers. [1]   The War Office, however, has not had the advantage of a naval type of organization and nomenclature for its factories as the Admiralty has for its dockyards, and it was therefore less easy to shift a man obviously and locationally from his skilled work to his unskilled.   In a dockyard a skilled labourer at the completion of his skilled work is shifted definitely into the " boatswain's gang."   In the Arsenal the change of occupation was often overlooked, and while doing labourer's work a man was paid on the skilled labourer's scale.   During 1908 this matter was dealt with, and it was decided to make the rate of pay depend strictly upon the type of work which the employee did.   The change is indicative of the movement from the old condition, in which pay depended upon status or rank rather than upon work done, to the newer idea akin to payment by results ;   but still the vested interests of the old hands were respected, and Mr. F. D. Acland, in a letter to the Labour Protection League, in March, 1909, announced that, " in view of the fact that some men have been drawing the higher rates continuously for some time, we are prepared to allow labourers appointed to the skilled ratings before the second of December, 1908, when the new order was issued, to retain those ratings." [2]   So far the action of the Department is perfectly just, but the occasion was seized as a chance to re-classify certain work, and to reduce the wages customarily given for it.   The re-arrangement also de-graded the old class of storehouse clerks to the position of skilled labourers—a change which was not only offensive in its new description to

---

[1] The problem of the skilled labourer is more fully treated in Chap. II and Appendix A.

[2] Letter published in " Woolwich Pioneer," March 19, 1908.

the clerical workers, but which further deprived them
of their privileges of leave-with-pay, and reduced their
rate of sick pay.   By a Departmental Order ten classes
of skilled labourers were re-rated as labourers, with
additional pay for their special work.[1]   In every case
the rearrangement meant a drop in wages—in the case
of the storehouse clerks to the extent of 2s. 4d. a week
—and the eventual saving to the Department on so
large a body of men was considerable.   Protests were
useless, and to the clerks the explanation given was
that the Admiralty got its clerical work in stores done

[1] Departmental Order, No. 5894 (January, 1908), was as
follows : " The undermentioned skilled labourers will in future
receive labourers' pay with additional pay at the following
rates :—

Skilled Labourers	Minimum		Maximum
Assistant Sawyer		Increment of 1d.	
(Canal Men)	2d.	per Diem Annually	6d.
,, Boilersmith ..	2d.	Do.	8d.
,, Bookbinder ..	2d.	Do.	8d.
,, Painter	2d.	Do.	8d.
,, Printer	2d.	Do.	8d.
Hammermen	2d.	Do.	8d.
Bottle Cleaner	2d.	Do.	4d.
Lubricator	2d.	Do.	4d.
Packers	2d.	Do.	4d.
Storehousemen	2d.	Do.	4d.
Clerical Duties in			
Storehouses	2d.	Do.	4d.

" A.   Subordinates now serving in ratings entitling them
to a higher maximum than 27s. per week to continue to be
eligible for such higher rate as a personal privilege.
   " B.   As a rule, one year to elapse before a fresh increment
is given.   On appointment a Skilled Labourer will not necessarily commence on the minimum rate of extra pay (2d. per
diem) ; the initial rate will be fixed in each case on appointment.   " (Sgd.) R. CRAWFORD,
                                              " For A.D.O.S."
" Woolwich Arsenal, 31.1.08.

by "unskilled labourers," and that the Treasury approved the action of the War Office in following that example.[1] Indeed, the Department itself seemed half ashamed of this action. Out of the negotiations on this subject there emerged one of the very few glimpses of direct pressure by the Treasury. "The Treasury," wrote Mr. F. D. Acland to Mr. Will Crooks, in July, 1907, " some time ago tried to make us abolish S.H.C. work in the storehouse altogether and have it done by writers in the central office." And later : " The War Office has not been able to retain the class of S.H.C. intact, for we have had to undertake that one-third of it shall gradually be replaced by skilled labourers as vacancies arise." [2] Hence the re-classification of 1908, inspired partly by the example of another Department, partly by the dictation of the Treasury, and partly by a desire for cheaper labour, while the workers were asking unceasingly that those terms which the War Office applied to its contractors it should adopt for itself.

Against the frequent charge that War Office wages were generally worse than those in private employment, it is common to advance the other advantages arising from employment under a Government Department. If continuity of employment be one of these, it is well to remember that until labour organization and representation became powerful enough to exert an influence in these matters, a change of Government not infrequently meant a change of policy in which the dismissal of thousands of workmen might be involved. After the Boer War the peace-time strength

[1] Letter from Mr. F. D. Acland to Mr. Will Crooks published in " Woolwich Pioneer," July 26, 1907.
[2] Ibid.

of Woolwich Arsenal was reduced by 6,000 men.[1] The introduction of the " feed and speed " system led to the discharge of many slow workers.[2] Piecework, prior to the agreement upon an " interim rate," often corresponded to short time when work was slack.[3] And always the danger existed of a re-classification of grades, with a consequent fall in earnings. The element of continuity, therefore, seems to have been hardly greater than that found in private employment. Certain privileges there were. They have since been valued and their value deducted from the " district rate." They bear, however, a very pale resemblance to the type of privilege which one is inclined to associate with Government employment generally. There was, and is, no possibility of a pension except for the supervisory ranks. The workers' plea for pensions on a contributory basis has even been refused. The gratuity, which may be obtained after seven years' service if the retirement of the workman is in consequence of the abolition of his post, or after fifteen years if he retires through ill health, consists of one week's pay for every year of service. Public holidays were generally four days in the year. Medical attendance at Woolwich was given in the Arsenal surgery, and sick pay was in most cases contingent upon a certificate from the department's doctor. After the lyddite explosion at Woolwich in 1903 men who absented themselves from work owing to shock were not placed on the sick-pay list unless they were receiving treatment at the Arsenal surgery.[4] The

[1] " Woolwich Pioneer," April 17, 1908.
[2] *Ibid.*, June 21, 1909.
[3] Subject to certain conditions time-wages are now guaranteed to persons paid by results.
[4] " Hansard," July 5, 1903.

system of making a deduction, either implicitly or avowedly, from wages to cover these privileges has never been wholly satisfactory, and up to the outbreak of war in 1914 it had been a standing grievance that the gratuity of a man who died while in the service of the War Department might not be drawn by his relatives.

The year 1912 saw the beginning of the general movement of wages towards their outside equivalent. On time work this was a comparatively straightforward proceeding. On piecework some of the difficulties have already been shown. It was largely because of the need of machinery to deal with rate-fixing questions that the shop stewards' agitation gained such strength. Application for permission to establish shop stewards in 1913 was flatly refused by the Army Council.[1] In 1914 came the strike at Woolwich Arsenal, which arose on a question of blackleg labour very remotely concerning the Arsenal, but which yielded the Woolwich workers many things, and among them the right to set up shop stewards. With a shop steward and shop committee for every fifty men this organization has formed a wonderful network through 130 shops in the Arsenal. Its especial care has been piecework rates. Low-priced jobs have been refused on behalf of a whole shop by the shop steward. Even there the work has not ended. " We found," said Mr. Jack Mills to the writer, " that a job refused in one shop would be taken away to another corner of the Arsenal and offered to another shop on the same terms. We have traced

[1] Letter from Mr. R. N. Brade (on behalf of the Army Council) to a Woolwich deputation, published in " Woolwich Pioneer," May 16, 1913.

several cases of that sort and prevented the acceptance of jobs at unfair prices. Where piecework has been underpriced we have got it raised, and often obtained the difference of back pay for the workers concerned. In some cases men have received from £14 to £26 back pay." Piecework thus has rendered almost obsolete the old Fair Wages Resolution except in so far as it still forms a basis on which to calculate the rate necessary to produce time and a third at piecework. Woolwich has met the new situation with its shop stewards. Other departments of the War Office are also more fortunately placed to-day, for their wages grievances are referable to the Joint Industrial Council (trade sections) of the War Office and ultimately to the Industrial Court. Woolwich so far has refused to submit its affairs to the Whitley Council machinery. It has been suggested that this is because the Woolwich workers fear a comparison of their terms with those of other War Office workers ; that they are afraid the other people would ask to be levelled up, and " the Government would do the levelling—down." This, however, would be an admission that Woolwich is in a favoured position, and that it has got there chiefly by exerting pressure of various kinds—that is to say, that War Office wages have depended in the past upon the bargain pure and simple, that those have fared best who were best equipped for bargaining, and that War Office wages are derived from no more ideal principles than are those which the action of the ordinary economic forces produces.

The problem of the War Office factories still exists. A large skeleton strength is still retained and has been criticized by the Geddes Committee on National Expenditure. Woolwich is too big, the Waltham factory is unnecessary, the general stigma of slack production is attached to Government establishments all round. The war has demonstrated the possibility of turning private plants on to munition work with great rapidity in time of emergency, and the question must arise as to the desirability of maintaining national factories on the scale at which they have been kept in the past.

This examination, however, yields some interesting conclusions. While it is undoubtedly true that the broad bases of wages in the past have rested upon supply and demand, there are indications of a tendency to value the worker first and the work second, which endured until piecework supervened and the " skilled labourer " system was adopted. There is a humanitarian flavour in this which one expects to find only among social reformers of to-day and not in the industrial methods of the past. It seems very much like an attempt to desert the ordinary commercial system and adopt a new one embodying principles which advanced labour theorists would urge at present. Especially interesting are the fact that the experiment failed and the reasons for that failure. In 1908 the War Office, pressed by the Treasury, had to pass from the old system to one which sought to relate pay to effort.[1] Economy, therefore, was the initial cause of its abandonment, and concurrently it must be remembered that the workers themselves never attempted to reassess values, or to look at the matter from any other angle than that of ordinary industry. They agitated throughout for wages which should approximate to those of private enterprise—an attitude which was taken up to meet the wage-cutting of the

[1] *Supra*, p. 21.

Department. It may be thus fairly concluded that the attempt to substitute for " payment for output " an ideal of decent maintenance in return for which service should be given failed because it was undesirable to both sides, and because, in practice, it did not yield to either employer or worker a favourable comparison with ordinary business methods.

CHAPTER II

THE ROYAL DOCKYARDS

IN the Royal Dockyards, as in the Arsenal and National Factories, much of the work is similar to that carried on under private control. Ship-building and ship-repairing constitute a trade in which wage-regulation has developed intricate machinery and has involved absolute recognition of the principle of collective bargaining. Such arrangements for the industry generally have had no reference to His Majesty's Dockyards until quite recently, and wage-fixing for Admiralty employees has certainly not proceeded along the lines laid down by negotiation for private shipyards.

The Admiralty, perhaps more than any other Government Department, has lived in an atmosphere of detachment from the outside world, and has conducted its affairs with an air of autocracy—not always undesirable, sometimes almost paternal, but invariably conservative. Its activities have been essentially and particularly its own. They have been planned on distinctive lines, have been located at points where the influence of similar undertakings was least strong, and have been sufficiently homogeneous to make individual organization easy in earlier days, powerful enough latterly to make successful attack most difficult. The Admiralty could never forget that it was pre-eminently the administrator of a Royal service. Many years of pressure were needed to convince it that it was chiefly, and for the most prolonged periods, an employer of labour, and was, only at long intervals and for brief spells, an active arm of the sovereign power. If My Lords Commissioners of the Admiralty could have forgotten this aspect of their business and have overlooked some of the century-old methods of their predecessors, they would have been far less harassed during the present century, and would have expended less effort and thought in the maintenance of a dignity which was not really threatened. They would also have avoided producing in their workers the sense of impotence, which only a war, with its judicial concessions and its semi-democratic aftermath, prevented from developing into an avowed challenge. Under this spell of sovereign direction fell all wages questions for many years. Employees might submit, at such times once a year as My Lords made their itinerary of the dockyards, petitions " humbly begging " that their wages might be increased, or hours of work shortened, or conditions altered. Matters of wider interest—matters which touched the workers as a class rather than as individuals —were outside the sphere even of petitions. Such affairs—minor matters of policy frequently, it is true —were the sole prerogative of the Commissioners. " Requests of this nature cannot be entertained," is a typical reply to a petition that the practice of giving out such work as sluice and stop-valves at Devonport be discontinued.[1] Or, again, the request that boat repair work be done in the Dockyard at Portsmouth

[1] Answers to Petitions (1908): Admiralty document C.N. 21716/09, Item 45.

instead of by contract was met with a similar formula :
" This matter is not admitted as a proper ground of
complaint on the part of workmen." [1] Even this
much, however, is a concession, for to state the reason
for refusing to grant a request is an extremely modern
proceeding. Until 1906, answers to petitions were
terse and brief, and the phrase " Not approved "
dismissed those upon which the powers could not look
favourably.

Thus it is only in comparatively recent years,
when the system had already suffered some buffetings,
that a glimpse is obtainable of the view taken by the
Admiralty on the mass of questions which the workers
were claiming as their concern. Men employed on
riveting and iron-caulking at Chatham, Devonport, and
Pembroke, who asked to be allowed " to collaborate
with officials in revising and drawing up piecework
schemes " in 1908, were flatly refused. [2] Others, who
asked that their wages should be raised because of
correspondingly higher rates paid in private yards,
were reminded that the Admiralty did not admit the
justice of basing wages on those paid for similar work
in other districts. [3] Even so straightforward a petition

[1] Answers to Petitions (1908) : Admiralty document
C.N. 21716/09, Item 83.

[2] Admiralty document C.N. 21716/09, Item 220. The
method in private industry, at this time was practically the
same as that asked for in the above petition. Piece prices
were fixed by the employers but were subject to negotiation
if challenged. " Any claim for alteration of price must be
made *before the commencement of the job* "—General Agreement
in Shipbuilding Trade, Sec. IV, quoted in Board of Trade
Report on Collective Agreements, Cd. 5366 of 1910.

[3] Admiralty document C.N.21716/09, Item 72. The reply
is : " Their Lordships are unable to accept the view that the
weekly rates of wages of Dockyard workmen should be
determined according to the weekly rates paid to workmen

as that of the Devonport skilled labourers, asking that they " be not removed from piecework to time-work unbeknown to them," was not answered with an assurance that care should be taken, but simply with the chilly announcement : " It is the practice to acquaint men with the conditions under which they are working." [1]   So, too, in the form signed by workmen in applying for appointment to established positions, unquestioning obedience is demanded.   In such application the worker is required to promise to obey the instructions of his superior officer, and to perform his duties on all such occasions as his superior officer may think necessary, and under such conditions " of rest and rates of payment as may from time to time be prescribed by the Admiralty." [2]   The last phrase perhaps most aptly sums up the attitude of the Commissioners to the question of industrial conditions. Wages, hours, and methods of organization are " prescribed."   They are not the result of joint agreement or collective bargaining.   They are determined by the Board of the Admiralty, and there they stand for every individual workman to accept or reject.   No middle course is open until, as has happened occasionally, the passive resistance of a whole class of workers has indicated the failure of the Admiralty to strike

of the same trade designation employed in some other district or districts without regard to differences in the conditions of the employment and in local circumstances.   Further, although when the Dockyard working week was reduced to 48 hours, no reduction was made in wages, no pledge was given, nor was it admitted tacitly or otherwise that the Dockyard workmen would in future be entitled to the same weekly rates of wages as workmen in the outside trade working 53 or 54 hours a week."

[1] Admiralty document S. 20602/13, p. 39.
[2] Admiralty Form D. 124.

a bargain. In such case the Admiralty " prescribed " again a little higher, and workers were attracted. The process was long and the delay awkward, but at least My Lords had preserved their sense of autocracy and had avoided anything so undignified as the haggling by which a bargain is *quickly* struck.

The same spirit has pervaded other matters which, in private industry, were admitted as subjects in which the men might participate. Demarcation troubles invaded the Royal Dockyards as they did the private shipbuilding trade, though in a less degree, for reasons which appear later. Nevertheless those which had to be dealt with were made no part of negotiations. The Admiralty constituted itself arbitrator, and in 1913 published a long document in which demarcation rulings were laid down. These had some regard to the customs adopted in the industry outside. Where there was no such guide, however, and the claims of different classes were incompatible, the arrangements were made with the object of getting the work done " with the greatest efficiency and the least dislocation of labour." [1] Slowly, but surely, this spirit of untrammelled control has relaxed during recent years, yet the attitude is still far from abandoned. An Admiralty official declared, with conviction, to the writer that the system of collective bargaining had never been acknowledged by the Board, though a Whitley Council meeting had just ended. Even in its best days this outlook was not without its good side. The Admiralty may have been an employer with decided views of its own and quite intolerant of interference, but it has also been an employer with a kindly feeling towards its workers on occasions—a sense which was not

[1] Admiralty document S. 20602/13 (Demarcation Scheme).

wholly unreciprocated. Indeed, the Ministry of Labour liaison officer on the Admiralty Joint Industrial Councils to-day feels almost like an outsider who is tolerated, but who, of course, cannot be expected to enter into the spirit animating those who are part of this huge machine. It is perhaps, then, with a half-paternal gesture that the Admiralty calls in its workers occasionally to some act of co-operation which looks well and means little. In this fashion a new scheme of workmen's compensation was submitted to a referendum of Dockyard workers in 1912. It improved the terms provided in the previous scheme, but after the vote every individual workman still retained the right to accept the new terms, or to elect to rely on the provisions of the Workmen's Compensation Act of 1906 ; and further, to enter or withdraw from the new scheme at any subsequent time. A huge vote of over 50,000 employees approved of the scheme.[1] In other respects the Commissioners have really been solicitous for the well-being of their workers. Overalls of some sort or other have, for many years, been issued to men when employed on work likely to be destructive of clothing ; and for work which might damage boots, or in which the workmen might get wet feet, clogs are supplied. The answer to an appeal by the electrical fitters at Sheerness for overalls when working on board ships is a note calling the attention of the yard officers to the regulation on the subject.[2] These regulations are most comprehensive. They authorize the provision of overalls to prevent damage to clothing ; fearnought dresses " for protection against weather or against exposure to extreme temperatures " ;

[1] Admiralty document S. 20602/13, p. 12.
[2] Ibid., C.N. 21716/09, Item 42.

waterproof clothing for "special duties"; and
waterproof boots or clogs when necessary and especially where men's boots are "liable to damage by
acids." [1] Such care for workpeople is wholly admirable.
And the sense of a *desire* on the part of the Admiralty
to deal fairly with its employees is obtained from the
verdict on its working of the premium bonus system.
Easy as it would have been to exploit the workmen
under this system, no attempt was made to do so.
The testimony of a joint committee of seven trades,
set up by the Trades Union Congress in 1910, to
investigate the matter is of interest. "The Committee regret the existence of the system in Government Dockyards," they reported, "but it is only fair
to acknowledge that it seems to be administered with
a fairness and humanity which are almost universally
absent outside the Service." [2]   Similarly, changes in
the arrangements for submitting petitions seem to
have been dictated by an intention to deal consider-
ately with the men.   A circular in September, 1913,
urged that grievances which needed immediate attention should be laid by the workers before the responsible
officials, and ordained that in matters concerning large
classes of men representatives might in future be
elected from among the workmen, who should be
granted interviews with the Financial Secretary in
London, and who should have their deputation
expenses paid by the Admiralty.[3]   By February, 1915,
the men had gained their point as to trade union
recognition, and were granted permission to send
with the elected deputies "other persons nominated

[1] Admiralty document D. 30925/14, p. 40.
[2] Monthly Report, Amalgamated Society of Carpenters and
Joiners, April, 1910 : Report of Joint Committee.
[3] Admiralty document S. 20602/13, p. 5.

3

by them and not exceeding half their [the deputies']
number," whose expenses would *not* be paid by the
Admiralty.[1]

Such line of action points to the willingness to make
the workers as comfortable as might be.   The same
spirit doubtless underlay the old petitions.   Further,
a mass of regulations, contained in several handbooks,
laid down rules for the guidance of the local officials
and provided for numerous contingencies.   These may
be justly compared with a written State constitution.
Its inelasticity caused friction ; and since industrial
conditions change at least as rapidly as those of a
nation, cases frequently arose which the regulations
did not cover.   It is true that annual visits to the
dockyards by the First Lord or his representative
kept the central authority in touch, to some extent,
with the realities, but the Admiralty was too remote
to have its finger continually on the pulse.   Considerable responsibility devolved upon the local official,
and, provided he did not exceed the regulations, there
was practically no check upon his interpretations,
except that constituted by the complaints of the
workmen.   It rested with the wage-earners to press
for the yard officers to keep conditions right up to the
standard which the Admiralty regulations allowed.

It was with this matter of local administration
that the Admiralty failed to grapple.   Already over-
whelmed perhaps with its own rules and regulations,
it apparently hesitated to add new ones which should
safeguard the workers.   In 1908 it was evident that
the responsible officers at Pembroke had been guilty
of something akin to sharp practice.   The shipwrights
in that yard petitioned that piecework rates " be not

[1] Admiralty document D. 30925/14, p. 5.

reduced without due notice being given," and the reply of My Lords was to quote an instruction which covered this.[1] On the other hand, evidence of the inability of a written constitution to provide against every contingency, and of the unreadiness of the local official to act intelligently when a new item arose, is to be obtained from a petition in the same year from the ship riggers of Chatham and Sheerness. Their request is worth quoting in full : " That wages may not be checked for mealtimes when men are ordered to work ' straight on ' and no mealtimes are allowed." [2] Though riggers might obligingly work from morning till night without a break in order to get a ship away, it had never appeared strange to the yard officers to deduct the usual mealtimes from the men's total of hours. The Admiralty upheld the men's request, and so added one more ruling to the already large list. Generally, however, the impression is gained that the Admiralty preferred to shelter behind its regulations, and the yard officials have been to a very great extent local arbiters. They decided when labourers employed on particular work might be classed as " skilled labourers " and paid higher rates.[3] They were responsible for advancing a certain proportion of tradesmen to wages above the minimum within limits laid down by instructions.[4] They determined under what conditions and for what periods confined space allowance and " risk money " were payable.[5] They were confirmed in their practice of deciding what joinery work should be given to joiners and what

[1] Admiralty document C.N. 21716/09, Item 74.
[2] *Ibid.*, Item 170.
[3] *Ibid.*, Item 216.
[4] Admiralty document S. 20602/13, p. 25.
[5] *Ibid.*, pp. 37 and 49.

to skilled labourers.[1] To them it was left to determine
when the work of skilled labourers engaged in driving
cranes and otherwise attending men engaged on
piecework involved piecework intensity and merited
extra pay.[2] Such questions as these inevitably
produced a crop of petitions every year. They were
of course merely matters of detail, but details of this
sort were capable of changing the complexion of the
Admiralty's intentions with regard to its workers.
The same lack of close touch is discernible in the
long-continued grievance that the relatives of a
worker who had qualified for a pension or gratuity
but had not retired before his death received nothing.
The Admiralty took refuge behind the Superannuation
Acts of 1859 and 1887, and it was not until the passing
of the Superannuation Act of 1914 that relief in this
respect was afforded.[3]

The remoteness of the controlling power defeated
the Admiralty's ideal of being the father of its people.
It seems never to have faced the possibility that its
children might grow up and develop new and
changing needs. Indeed, the one influence which the
Admiralty Commissioners most dreaded was change.
Their worst nightmare was that the labour arrangements should be subject to frequent changes, that
they should respond to varying conditions, that there
should be neither finality nor stability. They feared
a condition of flux. They would have much
preferred to remain isolated completely from the rest
of the industrial world. Outside industry could not
be held at arm's length. The Admiralty had to touch

---

[1] Admiralty document S. 20,602/13, p. 26.
[2] *Ibid.*, p. 36.
[3] Admiralty document D. 30925/14, p. 37.

it through the contractors who did part of their work. Admiralty employees touched it through the trade unions which desired to enrol them as members. The effect of this is to be seen in the attempt of the Board to compromise. It was not prepared to adopt outside standards for wage-fixing, but it was willing to compare its wages with those of private employers. An Admiralty official has declared to the writer that the ratio of the wages for various types of labour was determined by " settled relationships " established in private industry. Such relationships undoubtedly came, as far as actual craftsmen were concerned, from the customs of outside shipyards, but they provided simply a *ratio* and not a wage-figure. *Rates* of wages, pure and simple, were also compared, but at comparison the process had to stop, for the Admiralty decided that it must have uniform rates for similar grades in all dockyards in order that workmen might be moved at need from one yard to another. Nevertheless, questionnaires were sent to shipbuilding firms from time to time and information collected as to rates of wages in similar undertakings, and the Admiralty claimed that the " general level " of wages in the Royal Dockyards has been equal to the general level in outside yards.[1] When the period of Parliamentary indictment began in the early years of this century it also became the custom of the Parliamentary Secretary to the Admiralty to produce figures which purported to show that Admiralty wages were not far below those paid in private employment.[2] There is evidence, too, that in 1904 the

---

[1] Oral statement by Admiralty official.

[2] " Hansard," April 12, 1904. Mr. Pretyman said " he did not think the Admiralty would be justified in paying higher wages than private employers paid for similar work."

Board was busy collecting information from many quarters in consequence of the new tone of workers' petitions.[1] How far such comparisons were due to pressure of various kinds is not quite clear. At all events, agitation was beginning to manifest itself, and was soon to develop into a troublesome, if not formidable, element in dockyard wage questions.

The mere fact that the attack proceeded along the line of comparison with outside conditions is sufficient to show that Admiralty wages had not been based on those offered by the private employer. There were glaring discrepancies, even on a superficial examination. Some of them have not been wholly removed to-day, and they crop up regularly through a long period of years. One of the most striking and awkward—an attempt perhaps both to compromise on the matter of outside rates and to award recognition to workmen capable of the best work—existed in what was usually referred to as " classification in rates." In all trades and among semi-skilled workers a minimum rate was set, above which a fixed small proportion of men might be paid higher wages (at the discretion of the local officers), and in some rare cases a still higher wage was sanctioned for " special work." The higher rates frequently compared favourably with wages for similar work in private employment, but they were few and, from the men's point of view, arbitrarily awarded. Uniform rates for 1906 became a regular demand as an alternative to the request for the minimum to correspond with trade union rates.[2] The small proportion of men on

[1] " Hansard," July 29, 1904.
[2] Admiralty document C.N. 21716/09, Item 162, etc.

higher wages than the minimum may be gathered
from the following petition which was refused in
1912 :—" Skilled labourers. That 5 per cent. be
placed on maximum of 31s. per week." [1] Further,
the Admiralty claimed in some instances, in opposition
to claims for overtime payment, that workers' wages
had been so calculated as to constitute " inclusive
rates." [2] This contention was put forward to the
" yard craft men " (seamen, stokers, etc., on dockyard
tugs and launches) until 1915, though overtime at
a most generous rate was payable " only when
employees are doing work chargeable to private
individuals and other Government Departments." [3]
Even payment for supervision varied. The custom
was to pay a chargeman his usual trade rate plus
an allowance described as charge-pay of 6s. or 9s. a
week, according to the recommendation of the yard
officers. [4]

From 1904 the trade unions maintained a steady
opposition to the premium bonus system in the
dockyards, chiefly as a matter of principle, and in
1912 Mr. Winston Churchill, then First Lord of the
Admiralty, announced that it was to be abolished. [5]
The main assault on dockyard wages, however, was
pressed in the House of Commons. The chief champion
of dockyard workmen was Mr. Jenkins, member for
Chatham. In the debate on the Navy estimates of
1906 he condemned the skilled labourer system, by
which the Admiralty were getting done cheaply all

[1] Admiralty document S. 20602/13, p. 61.
[2] *Ibid.*, p. 26.
[3] Admiralty document D. 30925/14, p. 11.
[4] Admiralty document C.N. 21716/09, Item 198.
[5] Eleventh Quarterly Report, Parliamentary Committee,
Trades Union Congress, March, 1912.

kinds of work " which, when done by mechanics, receive the highest pay." [1] Mr. Summerbell (Sunderland) declared that the wages of sailmakers in the dockyards were only from 28s. to 29s. 6d., while the wages for similar work in London were 40s. 6d., in Liverpool 36s., and in other places 33s. 9d. to 36s.[2] Sir J. Baker (Portsmouth) followed with the assertion that wages paid in the Dockyard at Portsmouth to labourers and mechanics were 2s. or 3s. below the current rate for that locality.[3] So powerful indeed was this onslaught that, but for the acceptance by the Parliamentary Secretary to the Admiralty of part of the agitators' demands, Mr. Jenkins' resolution might conceivably have been passed. Its terms indicate the opinion of representatives of dockyard towns on Admiralty wages : " This House is of opinion that the Government, as model employers, should pay the workers in the dockyards not less than the standard trade union rate of wages paid for similar work in the district ; further, in order to maintain amicable relations between the heads of the respective departments and employees, the right of negotiation through the accredited representatives of the workmen should be at once recognized."[4] This resolution exceeded by a good deal the limits of the Fair Wages Resolution which was to be passed four years later. It was withdrawn only on the assurance of Mr. Edmund Robertson that the Admiralty accepted the spirit of the first part of the resolution.[5]

[1] " Hansard," March 1, 1906.
[2] *Ibid.*
[3] *Ibid.*
[4] *Ibid.*
[5] *Ibid.* Mr. Robertson said : " The Government also recognized in principle, that it was their duty to pay ' the trade union

The fulfilment of that promise was a far less easy matter for the Admiralty than the making of it by its spokesman. The Admiralty undoubtedly believed it could carry out its promise. The petitions of the men that year were filled with requests for trade union rates, and four months after the undertaking was publicly given Mr. Robertson again assured the House that those petitions would be dealt with " in the spirit of my statement in the course of the debate on March 1st." [1] In 1913 the engineering trades—most powerful and most successful of all the grades in the dockyards—were still urging the adoption of trade union rates, which would have involved, according to their estimate, a rise of 4s. 6d. for most of their members. [2] They even attempted to force home their claim by a strike which started at Devonport and spread to Chatham and Portsmouth, but achieved only a partial success. " The Admiralty," wrote one of the participants, " after much inquiry and many excuses, agreed to rise the minimum rate. Such rise only affected a small percentage of our men and still left such minimum 2s. below the contractors' men doing the same class of work in the same yards." [3] This was probably the first attempt of dockyard workers to enforce their demands. It has not been repeated. But it indicates definitely that the seven-year-old promise had not been redeemed. Nor has

rate of wages paid for similar work in the district,' but they coupled that with the condition that differences between dockyard and outside work must be taken into account."

[1] " Hansard," July 2, 1906 (answer to question by Mr. Jenkins).

[2] " A.S.E. Journal," October, 1913.

[3] *Ibid.*, August, 1913 : Letter from T. Proctor (Devonport).

it yet been completely fulfilled.   Absolute fulfilment would have meant the breaking of habits which have almost become traditions.

How little the organization and administration of a Royal dockyard have changed, in comparison with the change in its products and the advance in its equipment, is not realized until its wage-paying system is examined.   New machinery, tools and methods of work have been adopted and adapted.   The type of ship built, fitted, repaired, and refitted has changed every year.   The Admiralty clung tenaciously to its old system of employing labour, adding a new class occasionally, more often fitting an old class for a new type of work, with very slight regard to the independent economic value of such work.   Some engineers had to be imported when the steamship arrived ;   some boilermakers and iron shipbuilders, but only in so far as they were quite indispensable.   The Admiralty was already possessed of a mass of labour by which the less difficult portions of iron-work could be done after little instruction and practice.   This body of workmen, valuable to the Admiralty both for its adaptability and its cheapness, was retained intact and defended valiantly until 1917.   It was quite the greatest source of trouble to the trade unions and provided them with an awkward problem in their own ranks as well as constituting a most difficult industrial question.

It is interesting to inquire as to the types of work with which the " skilled labourer " was entrusted. In 1908 platers, riveters, drillers, and iron-caulkers were among the metal trade classes who were described as skilled labourers.[1]   Men engaged in making stages

[1] Admiralty document C.N. 21716/09, pp. 24 and 25.

in docks were similarly rated,[1] and even the work of electrical wiring was given to the same grade.[2] Crane-drivers, workers overhauling crane jibs, hammer-men, painters, and men " booking and transporting wireless stores " were included in the same list.[3] In 1912 the drivers of locomotives in the Works Department were added, and one worker at Devonport employed on " sun printing and photography " was actually described as a skilled labourer.[4] Still the list is incomplete. Crane attendants, dredgermen, the operators of punching and shearing machines, even telephone operators, are brought under this heading.[5] The employment of skilled labourers on these jobs has been steady and regular. Their trade, as such, has been engulfed in the convenient omnibus term " skilled labourer." Intermittently other work has been provided for out of this inexhaustible store. The minimum rate of pay for these workers in 1912 was 24s. per week (after one years' work on a " probationary rate " of 23s.). Wages above that figure were payable in certain circumstances for small percentages at the discretion of the local officials. The maxima for various types of work, however, ranged chiefly from 28s. to 31s.

An independent comparison of Admiralty rates for certain grades may be gained from the table on p. 44, which shows official figures for the year 1906.[6]

[1] Admiralty document C.N. 21716/09, p. 24.
[2] *Ibid.*, p. 26.
[3] Admiralty document S. 20602/13, pp. 38, 42, 46, 53, 58.
[4] *Ibid.*, pp. 53 and 62.
[5] Admiralty document D. 30925/14, pp. 44 and 56.
[6] Board of Trade Report on Earnings and Hours of Labour, 1906, Vol. VI (Cd. 5814 of 1911), pp. 59-124 ; and Board of Trade Report on Changes in Rates of Wages and Hours of Labour in 1906 (Cd. 3713 of 1907), p. 149.

Grade	Average in Private Employment		Wages of more than 50 per cent. of Private Hands	Admiralty.
	Lowest	Highest		
	s. d.	s. d.	s. d. s. d.	s. d. s. d.
Shipwrights ..	34 9	40 10	35 0–45 0	— 35 6
Caulkers[1]	37 2	67 0	45 0–80 0	22 0–28 0
Riveters[1]	46 0	61 9	50 0–80 0	22 0–28 0
Platers[1]	54 11	82 0	55 0–80 0	22 0–28 0
Patternmakers ..	34 6	43 10	35 0–45 0	34 0–45 0
Boilermakers (platers)	33 5	44 0	35 0–45 0	34 0–48 0
Sailmakers	30 4	35 0	— 35 0	— 30 6
Coppersmiths ..	33 10	43 0	37 5–43 0	34 0–42 0
Wheelwrights[2] ..	28 0	32 0	— 32 0	— 32 0

Theoretically, the skilled labourer had acquired his skill in the dockyard, and in many cases this was true. Nevertheless, a craftsman engaged for any of these classes of work became a skilled labourer for purposes of rating and pay. It was also the theory of the Admiralty that this system was essential to the success of their efforts to preserve continuity of employment. When work for which the skilled labourer was specially fitted fell short, he was not to be "stood off" but transferred to the boatswain's gang as an ordinary labourer, receiving a labourer's pay. Not always was it clear when a man graduated from labourer to skilled labourer, and the reply of the Commissioners to one appeal in 1912, was: "The Yard Officers must decide in which particular cases the rating of Skilled Labourer may appropriately be given in accordance with general Admiralty instructions." [3] The real trouble, however, was that work

[1] Figures in the first three columns represent piecework earnings.

[2] "Report on Earnings and Hours of Labour," 1906, Vol. VIII, p. 250.

[3] Admiralty document S. 20602/13, p. 36.

which outside the dockyards constituted a skilled trade was given to non-craftsmen and paid for at rates below the value of such work in private industry. From this point of view the question was attacked for more than a decade.

The House of Commons in 1904 saw the opening of the attack,[1] and it was taken up and continued by the Trades Union Congress down to the beginning of the war. Resolutions of condemnation were passed annually, and deputations from the Parliamentary Committee of the Congress appeared before every successive First Lord to urge the abandonment of the system. In 1908 Mr. D. C. Cummings (boilermakers) told Lord Tweedmouth that the wages of ironworkers in the dockyards were " at least 20 to 25 per cent. below those paid in the private yards of the country for time-workers, and probably 40 to 50 per cent. for piece-workers." [2] In 1911 Mr. J. Hill (boilermakers) made similar representations to Mr. McKenna. The work of pinching, shearing, bending, riveting, caulking was paid for as skilled work in private shipyards, " even in the building of a tramp." The men who did that work were " looked upon as tradesmen and classed as such." The final denunciation is expressed in this further remark of Mr. Hill: " Their wages are at least 10s. per week higher than the wages paid to your ' skilled labourers.' " [3] In the same interview Mr. J. Jenkins taunted the First Lord with the small volume of work put out on contract. " You have to

[1] " Hansard," February 29, 1904 : Speeches of Captain Norton and Mr. Kearley.

[2] Report of Parliamentary Committee, Trades Union Congress, March, 1908.

[3] Eighth Quarterly Report, Parliamentary Committee, Trades Union Congress, March, 1911.

pay," he said, " 36s. or 39s. to the men outside, and
yet in your own dockyards men are working for 23s.
or 28s. or an average of 25s., per week." [1]   Again in
1912 the case was submitted to Dr. Macnamara,
then Parliamentary Secretary to the Admiralty.   This
time Mr. Hill actually advanced a threat that the
trade unions would cut down the supply of skilled
labourers by permitting them to move as craftsmen
to private dockyards.   " We could take," he said,
" thousands of your men from the Royal Dockyards.
There is a considerable shortage of riveters and
caulkers in the private dockyards and shipyards, and
if we decided to take them there would certainly be
a shortage of labour." [2]

The effect produced on the Admiralty by such
efforts as these was *nil*.   Lord Tweedmouth defended
the system on the ground that it conduced to
continuity of employment.[3]   Mr. McKenna argued that
of all the 10,000 skilled labourers then (1911) employed
by the Admiralty few had been for any length of time
engaged on one class of work only.   He also advanced
the continuity theory. [3]   Dr. Macnamara, most sympathetic of Admiralty officials, defended the classification on similar grounds, advanced the strong point
that most of the workers concerned had served no
apprenticeship, suggested that the supply of labour
proved the wages to be adequate, and reminded the
trade union leaders that the men concerned would

[1] Eighth Quarterly Report, Parliamentary Committee,
Trades Union Congress, March, 1911.
[2] Eleventh Quarterly Report, Parliamentary Committee,
Trades Union Congress, March, 1912.
[3] Report Parliamentary Committee, March, 1908.
[4] Eighth Quarterly Report, Parliamentary Committee,
March, 1911.

not be accepted by the unions as the equals of men who had been apprenticed.[1] There was justice in this last argument, for when, in 1912, the question of admitting men of the skilled labourer class to the Boilermakers' Society was raised, keen opposition was offered by the members, and a vote taken in October, 1912, showed a majority of two to one against admitting them. Not until May, 1914, after much pressure by the dockyard men themselves, was the ruling reversed and skilled labourers accepted as members.[2] It might of course be urged that the wage and status, and not the skill, of these men rendered them undesirable to union members. It probably had the effect of strengthening the Admiralty in its belief that its treatment of these men was just. At all events it stood firm and no change whatever was conceded until 1917 : then only riveters, caulkers, and drillers were raised. They received an increase of 6s. in their basic rate and were elevated to the grade of mechanic. Other types of skilled labourers remained and are

[1] Eleventh Quarterly Report, Parliamentary Committee, March, 1912.
[2] "Boilermakers' Monthly Journal," September and October 1912, and March to June, 1914. The rules of the United Society of Boilermakers and Iron and Steel Shipbuilders, reissued in 1919, still contain the following provision as to the qualifications of candidates for membership :—
" The person proposed shall have worked not less than five years continuously at the trade previous to arriving at the age of 23 years as an apprentice. Any candidate who completes his apprenticeship according to the apprenticeship agreement, at any time previous to becoming 23 years of age, can be admitted as a first-class member, providing he has arrived at the age of 20. . . . The candidates must be efficient workmen and of good moral character. No person shall be proposed a first-class member of this Society over the age of 30 years."—Rule 21, Sec. 1.

still doing work which in many cases is strictly the work of a craftsman.

In considering these matters the impression steadily grows that the greatest obstacle to any improvements which would have brought the dockyards more into line with outside industry, and would have made for smooth relations with the workers, was the conservatism of the Admiralty. Through all its changes of work the Admiralty has striven to retain its old organization. Shipwrights, for instance, were until quite recent times all the workmen who "wrought on a ship," and the grade still includes several trades. Also the shipwrights still work in gangs. The spirit of the past is not easily eradicated. As long ago as 1905 Mr. Benn was urging in the House of Commons the need for the establishment of machinery to facilitate industrial negotiations in the dockyards.[1] We have seen how long that took to emerge. Complaints against the old methods came frequently from the men. Because the shipwrights remained a distinctive body, their pay also remained unchangingly distinctive, and applications in 1908 to be paid "trade rates" were refused.[2] Piecework found its way with comparative ease into the dockyards, but the conception of the extra effort involved by the attendance of time-workers on men paid by results was long considered before it was acknowledged. Numerous examples are to be found in the petitions of 1912. Men engaged on such work as crane-driving or "riming holes in front of riveters" had the greatest difficulty in convincing My Lords that they

[1] " Hansard," March 13, 1905 : " He suggested the establishment of something like a trade council."

[2] Admiralty document C.N. 21716/13, Item 72.

worked at piecework intensity when " attending on pieceworkers."

Largely because of the insistence of the Admiralty on the retention of its old methods of organization there undoubtedly was and still is, some foundation for the claim that Admiralty establishments may not fairly be compared with private shipbuilding or ship-repairing undertakings. That claim has been put forward by every First Lord since the question of fair wages was first raised. All the dockyards are differently organized from those of private enterprise, but surely the onus of justifying the difference should rest upon the Admiralty. All attempts at justifi-cation have rested upon two bases—the imperative need, in a national undertaking, of stability ; and the desire to secure for the workmen continuity of employment. The first alone has not been very convincing. As to the extent to which the second has been achieved some evidence will be considered later. No serious attempt has been made to justify the conditions on the ground that they pressed less heavily on the workers than those of private employ-ment. Whatever may be alleged as to the value of other advantages which Government service generally brings, it can scarcely be shown that wages under the Admiralty have been equal to those under the private employer. If it is true that wages differ from outside wages because of different arrangements, it seems equally true that they have differed, as a rule, for the worse. In 1905 Mr. Benn, speaking in the House of Commons, gave comparative figures which were by no means favourable to the Admiralty. He showed that joiners in shipbuilding yards on the Thames, Tyne, Mersey, Clyde, and in Belfast received

4

£2 for a week of 51½ hours, while those in Government yards were paid 32s. 6d. for a 48-hour week. He also maintained that the average wages of men engaged in " the hardware side of shipbuilding " in the dockyards were 6s. 6d. below those of workers in private yards.[1] In 1906 Mr. Jenkins contended that the Admiralty's own figures showed that they were paying 10 per cent. less than trade union rates.[2] Labourers at this time were paid 19s. a week, which, at Portsmouth for instance, was 2s. less than the current rate for the locality.[3] The methods of paying for overtime were severely criticized in 1907, when an instance was produced of an Admiralty writer at Chatham who, during a given period, worked 60 hours overtime and received pay for only 16 hours.[4] In later years the tale is very similar. Joiners were still complaining in 1908 that their wages were 4s. below the standard rate,[5] and ordinary labourers at Portsmouth claimed that the type of work they did was worth more than unskilled labourers' pay.[6] Seamen, stokers, etc., engaged on Dockyard tugs were appealing in vain for overtime to be paid for after 70 hours had been worked in any week, and this although the wage of a stoker, including provision allowance, was only 3s. 11d. a day.[7] In 1909 joinery work in the fitting up of offices at Keyham was given to skilled labourers at 2s. 6d. a week less

---

[1] " Hansard," June 29, 1905.
[2] *Ibid.*, December 10, 1906.
[3] *Ibid.*, March 1, 1906 : Speech by Sir J. Baker.
[4] Speech by Mr. H. H. Elvin (General Secretary N.U.C.), reported in " Woolwich Pioneer," November 29, 1907.
[5] Admiralty document C.N. 21716/09, Items 131 and 138.
[6] *Ibid.*, Item 287.
[7] *Ibid.*, Items 260 and 265.

than the trade price.[1] Piecework rates generally
were advanced in 1913, in order to maintain the ratio
between piece-prices and time-rates, which had been
increased. The piecework prices for plating on ships
were increased in all by 7 per cent., but when such work
was done by skilled labourers the percentage increase
allowed was only 4 per cent.[2] At the same time
complaints arose that earnings in excess of time-
rates on one job were being set off against earnings
which fell below time-rates on other jobs.[3] The
custom was condemned by the Admiralty (except
where the under earnings were " due to culpable
default "). Riggers brought forward the grievance of
being called into the Dockyard for a short job on
Sundays and of being paid only for the bare working
time.[4] Throughout, skilled labourers were asking for
trade rates, crane drivers in 1912 begging that their
minimum might be raised to 26s.[5] Apart from these
straightforward issues, the question of wages paid to
pensioners existed. In this matter the Admiralty
laboured like all other Government Departments under
the weight of a Treasury instruction which provided
that a deduction of at least 10 per cent. should be
made from the wages of men in receipt of a Government pension. This, however, could not have ac-
counted for the vast difference of wages in a case
noticed by the A.S.E. A large cantilever crane was
purchased by the Government from the Thames
Ironworks Company and installed at Chatham. A

[1] Monthly Report of the Amalgamated Society of Carpenters
and Joiners, May, 1909.
[2] Admiralty document S. 20602/13, p. 13.
[3] Ibid., pp. 39 and 40.
[4] Ibid., p. 2.
[5] Ibid., p. 58.

wage of £2 15s. had been paid by the Ironworks Company to the mechanic in charge, but at Chatham the naval pensioner doing the same work on the same crane received 28s.[1]

With regard to wages actually received, it is evident that the distinctive system of the Admiralty did not favour the workers, in comparison with outside employment. When dockyard wages are criticized on broad lines, however, attention is usually directed to the advantages represented by pensions, sick pay, and holidays. The two latter are of less importance than the pensions, or, at least, than the pensions would be if they were applicable to a majority of the workers. At any one time only one-third of the strength of a dockyard may be borne " on the establishment." Before the war the proportion was 25 per cent. Pensions, it should be remembered, are partially contributory. Deductions from wages in respect of pension prospects have been made for many years, the minimum being 1s. for men receiving 30s. and less, and rising by 6d. per week for every 6s. of wages above that figure. Since pensions are calculated on the wages which a workman has been entitled to during his service, the system has an element of justice, but even this had to be watched by the workers, for with the advent of piecework came the practice of estimating the pensions deduction on the piece-work earnings of the men and not simply on the time-rate to which their grade entitled them.[2] Having regard to the fact that deductions are made, vain efforts have been made by the workers to persuade

[1] " A.S.E. Journal," June, 1913 : Report of Organizing Delegate, No. 9 District.
[2] Admiralty document C.N. 21716/09, Item 78.

the Admiralty to calculate pensions on the " hired " rates of wages, i.e. on the wages rate *before* the pension deduction was made. For the refusal of this one can find no justification whatever. So the rule stands, nevertheless, and the maximum pension is forty-sixtieths of a man's pay after the pension contribution has been deducted. Since 1896 permission has been given to count half of a worker's " hired " service towards his pension, but the suggestion that all hired service should count has been summarily rejected. In 1912 My Lords took great trouble to point out that under existing conditions workmen who were placed on the established list had an advantage over those who were left on the hired list until late in their service, whereas if the men's request were conceded it would pay a worker to remain on the hired list until the last few years of his service.[1] Pensions, then, are of value to many of the Admiralty's servants, but no evidence is available as to the extent to which they are really privileges rather than advantages accruing from contributions by the workmen.

Since the National Health Insurance Act came into operation sick pay has ceased to be a considerable item, except in connexion with the Admiralty scheme for accident compensation, substituted for the terms of the Workmen's Compensation Act. Clearly, then, the privileges upon which a money value might be set are not large. Pensions, of course, are not wholly covered by the contributions of the men, but, as the men have frequently pointed out, the system is of great value to the Admiralty in binding to them a large body of indispensable workmen, who are peculiarly amenable to the discipline of the dockyards

[1] Admiralty document, S. 20602/13, p. 11.

In all and any of these matters the spirit of conservatism dies slowly. It is only necessary to look at the criticisms of the old petition system and to remember for how many years trade union leaders have growled their disapproval of the " cap in hand " process. Much agitation too was expended before permission was granted in 1912 for dockyard workers to be given leave in order to attend trade union meetings.[1] It was not until 1915 that men responsible for boilers and fires could secure any extra payment for the time spent after working hours in " pumping up boilers and drawing fires." [2] Also, it was only in 1912 that any attention was paid to the cost of living and its variations in different districts. Up to that time the craze for absolute uniformity had made wages in London the same as those for similar work in Devonport or Haulbowline. An additional 2s. per week was given to workers in the London area in 1912.[3] That difference has since been maintained, and during the war Haulbowline was rated generally at 1s. a week less than the ordinary dockyards of Great Britain. Nothing less disturbing than the war could have brought about any recognition by My Lords of the undisguised principle of collective bargaining, or could have secured the adoption of conciliation machinery. The answers to petitions issued from Whitehall in February, 1915, contained an unqualified refusal to the following not very revolutionary request :
" To arrange for the formation of a piecework prices board to consist of an equal number of officials and elected representatives of the workmen, and that no

[1] " Boilermakers' Journal," February, 1912.
[2] Admiralty document D. 30925/14, p. 44.
[3] Admiralty document S. 20602/13, p. 42.

prices be made or altered until considered and
approved by such board."¹ The end of the war
brought for the Admiralty, as for other branches of
the Government Service, a scheme of Whitley Councils,
but even to-day the decision of a Joint Industrial
Council is a unanimous agreement, or, failing that,
a reference to the Industrial Court. No vote is taken
to decide a particular line of action. If the matter
is not "agreed," other means of settlement are
immediately brought into operation.²

Thus the Admiralty is still very considerably a law
unto itself. It insists, of necessity, on the payment
of "district wages" by its contractors. Because of
its own need for uniformity of wages throughout its
dockyards it would claim that the same rule cannot
be applied to itself. A serious breach in this theory
was made when London and Haulbowline were given
special treatment, but already before that, the plan
had broken down and fitters, turners, boilermakers,
stonemasons, painters, and labourers in the Works
Department were paid less than similar ratings in
the "Vote 8" Departments, or dockyards proper.³
It is evident, too, that in all these matters a keen eye
was kept on cost. This, in view of Parliamentary
criticism, was inevitable ; yet it seems a poor argument
against raising wages which are manifestly below the
market rate to point out that the cost would be some
thousands of pounds. Mr. Pretyman, Parliamentary
Secretary in 1904, apparently regarded it as a con-
clusive answer to those who would have him improve
the condition of the skilled labourer, when he explained

¹ Admiralty document D. 30925/14, p. 53.
² See Chap. V, p. 141.
³ Admiralty document S. 20602/13, p. 52.

that wages in the dockyards were " so finely graduated that a rise in the lowest scale must carry with it increase over the whole area of wages," and that to give the labourers an advance of 1s. would cost about £10,000 a year, while to give an additional 1s. a week to all the workmen would cost £104,000. [1]   The same spirit appears in the answer to an appeal from electrical station supervisors in 1908 that annual leave might be granted without loss of pay. The reply was : " This request could not be granted without stopping payment for overtime " [2]—a dictum very similar to the Civil Service contention that it is not only right but beneficial for an officer to do a colleague's work during the holiday season (even if it lengthens his hours) without extra pay. Again, up to 1913 a reduction of 4 per cent. from the piecework rates of drillers was made on account of the grinding of tools,[3] and until 1915 men employed on the " yard craft " could get no payment at all for overtime. The concession, when made, allowed overtime payment only after a 12-hour day.[4]

Not all of these cases perhaps are typical, but they tend to support the sense that the cost of things often stood in the way of justice, and certainly of generosity. Some means of securing that the worker gave value for money was undoubtedly needed. " The dockyard stroke " was, before the war, a familiar synonym among manual workers for a job carried out in leisurely fashion and without undue exertion ; and one instance, at least, of the Admiralty's endeavouring to cope with such an evil may be gathered

---

[1] " Hansard," April 12, 1904.
[2] Admiralty document C.N. 21716/09, Item 125.
[3] Admiralty document S. 20602/13, p. 37.
[4] Admiralty document D. 30925/14, p. 11.

from a pronouncement on the payment of danger and confined space allowances in 1915. " As regards the complaint as to cutting down the number of hours for which the allowance is paid," the Commissioners wrote, " it should be understood that the time shown in the Recorder's diary to be charged to particular jobs in the Expense Accounts, is not the basis for the payment of allowances. The allowances are payable on the certificate of the Professional Supervising Officers as to the hours *necessarily* worked under the exceptional condition warranting the extra payments." [1] Since the war the charge of slackness has been advanced by the Geddes Committee in their complaint that the ratio of wages to material used is higher by 100 per cent. in the Royal dockyards than in private yards doing naval work. If the existence of the evil is admitted it would seem to be a foolish policy to meet it by paying less than current wages, rather than by paying full wages and insisting rigorously on decent effort in return.

The objection to the latter course is that an established workman can not have the threat of dismissal held over his head. Custom has certainly produced that difficulty, and for workers on the establishment the degree of continuity is practically absolute. In some degree the danger of dismissal which exists for the hired man is also small. But events have proved that dockyard workmen are not secure ; and since changes of policy in the past have produced heavy reductions in the dockyards, it is quite fair to assume that future rearrangements may also displace large numbers of workers. In March, 1906, Mr. Jenkins, in the House of Commons, accused the

[1] Admiralty document D. 30925/14, p. 41.

Admiralty of making the practice as winter approached of dismissing 1,500 men in batches from Portsmouth Dockyard.[1] The degree of fluctuation in general may also be gathered from the statement of Mr. Edmund Robertson in the same year, that between the years 1900 and 1906 the numbers of men employed in the dockyards had varied from 35,676 to a minimum of 27,000.[2] The Commissioners themselves in 1912 admitted the necessity of " standing off " such grades as painters during the winter. " Every effort," they wrote in answer to a petition, " is made to equalize the painting work over the year, but outdoor painting must be done to a greater extent during the summer months."[3] Other outdoor workers, too, suffered loss of time owing to bad weather.[4] These facts are an interesting commentary on the plea that the retention of the skilled labourer classification renders continuity of employment possible, but particularly they dispose of the claim that wages in the dockyard may be lower than outside because they are regular. For certain definite periods they would be found to be more regular than those of private employment. But when the break comes and some thousands of men are dismissed from one dockyard, the hardship is considerably greater than when work slackens in a private shipyard. There is no possibility of absorption in a dockyard town, and to obtain work the unfortunate mechanic or artisan must move to a distant port. His expenses in the course of the transfer would undoubtedly set off the advantage represented by the six or seven years' steady work which he has enjoyed.

[1] " Hansard," March 1, 1906.
[2] *Ibid.*, July 9, 1906.
[3] Admiralty document S. 20602/13, p. 53.
[4] *Ibid.*, p. 50.

It is impossible, then, to claim for the Admiralty
that its wages generally have been better than, or
even as good as, those of private industry. The
Board has stood alone and insisted on maintaining
its isolation. At the back of its present distinctiveness there operates very probably an influence which
arose from geographical isolation. Every dockyard
was established at a point far from the centres of
similar industry. Portsmouth, Devonport, Chatham,
Pembroke were all for many years in the heart of the
country—centres of work wholly separate and apart
from anything else in the vicinity. To say that the
Admiralty set them up is misleading in two senses.
It did not transport masses of labour from other
parts of the country to these new points, nor did
it establish dockyards in the form in which we know
them to-day. In all cases, except a war-time product
like Rosyth, the dockyards grew from small depots.
The Admiralty took for the most part the labour
which it found on the spot, and moulded and adapted
it to the growing requirements. Towns, around the
dockyards expanded, and without any voluntary
effort on the part of the Admiralty a very fair labour
supply was always available. Shipwrights were often
produced by families ; builders, masons, plumbers,
and the like are to found in any town. Only when
the iron ship and steam propulsion arrived to demand
new types of labour had My Lords to *attract* men to
their ports. Engineers had to be offered wages which
three-quarters of a century ago were high in comparison
with private industry. Having been attracted they
became victims of the fatal isolation, and even their
wages did not keep pace with those of their fellows
outside. In recent times the same difficulty has

been no less an obstacle.   It was useless for the House
of Commons to pass its Fair Wages Resolution in
1910, for " district rates " could have no meaning in
a dockyard.   Still the problem remains unsolved.
Trade union vigilance and agitation is doing something
to modify the autocracy which has characterized
Admiralty dealings with labour.   Nevertheless, dockyard labour remains a matter apart.   Trade unionism
has been wholly unwelcome, chiefly because it involved
contact with outside labour.   When the Government
began to show signs of adopting Whitley principles
for its own concerns the Admiralty sought to get in
first with a scheme based on direct representation
of the workers, and not on indirect representation
through the trade unions.[1]   The trade unions successfully opposed that, but they had a still more
difficult situation when, in connexion with the
moulders' strike of 1920, some dockyard members
of the Ironfounders' Society were called out.   The
Admiralty does not admit the right of an established
employee to strike, and its attitude in this case was
rigid.   The strikers were removed from the established
list, and but for trade union intervention would
probably have been discharged.

As a whole, the study of Admiralty wage-fixing
provides much support for the contention that wage
questions must generally be approached from the side
of historical inquiry rather than of theoretical analysis.
The distinctive characteristics of Admiralty labour
organization are only intelligible in the light of historical interpretation, and can only be justified or condemned by an examination of their results over a long
period.   Theoretically it might have been concluded that

[1] See Chap. V, pp. 142-4.

the Admiralty system would succeed, for it appears to have embodied the socially desirable principles of continuity of employment and the utilization of the same men through successive technical changes. Actually the scheme failed and the reasons for its failure are to be gathered only after experience. The pressure of the need for economy led the Admiralty to exploit its advantages and reduce wages for particular work, while on the other hand the workers were not prepared to forgo the chances of high gain, as seen in private employment, in return for the greater regularity of income offered by the Admiralty. That is to say that the scheme, good as it appeared in theory, had flaws which an attempt at working could alone reveal; and it points to the conclusion that economic forces from both sides—that of the worker and that of the employer—must be carefully reckoned with in schemes which seek to remove the disadvantages of the workers.

CHAPTER III

THE CIVIL SERVICE

TO pass to a consideration of the Civil Service is practically to leave the sphere in which comparisons with the conditions in private industry are possible. Only in its official description is this labour really similar to anything outside, if the lowest grades are excluded. Typists and routine clerks, of course, have their counterparts in ordinary employment, but for the grades above that the term " clerical labour " is a misnomer. The work of the civil servant should be more properly described as " administrative." It is becoming less a matter of routine and more a class of employment in which initiative and intelligence are called for. Upon its efficiency depends the ability of the State to keep national affairs moving smoothly, and this special importance gives to the Service a status entirely different from anything else the nation can show. Thoroughly able men are needed, and attention should be given to keeping workers efficient throughout their service. To what extent Treasury systems of wage-fixing have met this need will appear later. It is only necessary to state at once that the wage problems which the Service raised were distinctive and received distinctive treatment.

Since 1860 recruiting for the Civil Service has been chiefly carried on by the open competition system.

Prior to that time posts in the service of the State had been allotted by patronage, and the inevitable result of such privileges in the hands of Ministers and heads of departments was that the quality of work done frequently did not correspond to the price paid for it. For the last three-quarters of a century the process of nomination has filled far fewer posts than that of competition. The ideal at which administrators have aimed latterly, therefore, has been the securing of the best talent available ; and it is only from the point at which this change took place that salaries may be considered in the light of remuneration for work done or services rendered to the State. Previously such appointments were often a part of political strategy or rewards for party loyalty.

The scheme of competition brought with it its own difficulties, such as could only be met by a most painstaking and detailed organization. It may be justly assumed that every State department has its own special and peculiar work to do. That being so it would be reasonable that staffs for different offices should be chosen with regard to the special nature of the work. The attempt to adapt open competition to such requirements was never made, and so was avoided the need for grappling with two awkward problems—that of supplying departments with officials fitted for their work, and that of appraising relative work-values in many different sections of the administration. By 1914 there were (exclusive of the Post Office, Dockyards and Arsenal) 80 departments of the public service, employing 35,000 established and 25,000 unestablished servants.[1] Since then the number

[1] Fourth Report, Royal Commission on Civil Service (Cd. 7338 of 1914), par. 5.

of departments has been added to, and the total of employees has multiplied rapidly. Still the methods of the Civil Service Commissioners of half a century ago hold good, and the principles of recruitment, with but slight modifications, are maintained.

For the purposes of employment the service of the State is divided into three sections, which are broadly termed " administrative, clerical, and routine." Theoretically it is held that education in its fullest sense can inculcate the capacity for assuming responsibility, for acting individually, and for exercising the tact necessary in administrative work. To the class which is most highly educated, therefore, must go the positions which are loosely labelled " administrative." The age of eligibility was so fixed as to allow for the fullest normal education, and the nature of the competition was such as to demand, almost inevitably, a complete university course in preparation. Similarly with the second division, educational accomplishments which had no direct bearing upon the work subsequently to be performed decided largely the selection of candidates. For the routine work of the " assistant clerks " no high educational standard was demanded, but the process of examination was retained as preferable to anything which might smack of the old patronage or nomination system.

In all these cases the method of engaging labour was based upon a system which had only a vague relation to the fitness of the candidate for the particular work he would have to do. So, too, in regard to salaries, no estimate was placed upon the actual work to be carried out. The money value was placed rather upon the educational qualifications of the individual, or class of individuals

In theory, therefore, a great sameness must have been regarded as pervading all State work of a certain grade, or else all workers of a certain educational standard must have been regarded as capable of a vast range of occupations. Neither theory is quite true to the facts. The determination of the Civil Service Commissioners has evidently been to secure " the best brains of the nation." A decision of the Treasury to give persons who entered the first division a scale of pay with a wide gap between minimum and maximum fitted well into the scheme of things, and made it possible for such young men to be engaged in work of a semi-apprentice nature in the early years of their service. By this means the State secured a body of well-educated young men whose mental abilities they proceeded to adapt to specialized conditions. The result has not been unsatisfactory.

Under such conditions the most important qualification for the highest State employment did indeed become education, and the Royal Commission which reported in 1914 gave its support to the existing method. " We believe," they said, " that for men who are later to be engaged in administrative work a four to six years' course of the highest education between the years of 18 and 22, and over, constitutes a much better preparation than four to six years spent in junior clerical work, and that therefore the initial salary given to those who enter by the Class 1 examination should be high enough to encourage them to take that course, instead of entering the service at the earlier age." [1]

Hence, salaries, for the first division at all events, were to be regulated upon a supply and demand basis,

[1] Fourth Report, Royal Commission on Civil Service, (Cd. 7338 of 1914), par. 43.

5

and part of the remuneration might be looked upon
as interest on money expended in securing education.
For the second division also a similar allowance,
reduced in a sort of proportion to the educational
standard required, was made ; while for the lower
rank the wage basis seems very much to have hovered
round the subsistence level. In fact, the initial salary
of £45 for an assistant clerk in 1913 was certainly below
the market rate, though it was of course compensated
for to some extent by pension and sick leave privileges.

The salaries of all three grades were determined
with close reference to market values. The Royal
Commission of 1914 declared that first division
candidates must have prospects offered to them,
which were on the whole " equally eligible " with those
offered them in the open professions.[1] And again
in considering salaries for the new " junior clerical
class " which it proposed, the Commission made
recommendations after weighing the evidence taken
" as to the practice of some typical commercial
and industrial enterprises."[2] In the case of such
highly qualified workers as analytical chemists, employed by the War Office, it was maintained before
the Commission that the salaries were insufficient to
attract the best men in the future, and Sir William
Ramsay expressed the opinion that the War Office
would have to pay more if it was to continue to get
its work done well.[3] Sir Edward Troup (Home
Office), discussing the wages of factory inspectors'
clerks at £60 to £100, said : " If we want to increase

[1] Fourth Report, Royal Commission on Civil Service
(Cd. 7338 of 1914), par. 43.
[2] Ibid., par. 21.
[3] Second Appendix to Fourth Report, Royal Commission
on Civil Service (Cd. 7340 of 1914), Q. 22,577.

their salaries, we must go to the Treasury for more money, and I think we should have to be in a position to say that we could not get satisfactory clerks at the existing salary before the Treasury would agree to increase the amount. I do not think that a mere expression of opinion that the salary is insufficient would carry weight. I am bound to say, however, that I think the initial salary now given to assistant clerks is too small." [1] The supply and demand test seems to be the only one applied consistently. Sir William Ramsay suggested to the Commission that salaries should be commensurate with the social class of the officers concerned[2]—a combination apparently of the standard of comfort and cost of living on an individualist basis. It is evident that the cost of living had had very little effect on remuneration up to 1914, for the salaries of medical inspectors of the L.G.B. were not revised between 1887 and 1913, nor were those of Government analysts between 1894 and 1913.[3]

It is particularly in regard to the salaries of women that adherence to market price is most clearly seen. Great disparities in the rates for women and men doing similar work are to be found. One instance which may be quoted is that of shorthand writers. The salaries of the men in 1913 were from £104 to £300, while the women received from 26s. to 31s. per week.[4] Also the Secretary of the Post Office (Sir Alexander King) assured the Royal Commission that the disproportion in wages in the Post Office depended

[1] Appendix to Second Report, Royal Commission on Civil Service (Cd. 6535 of 1914), Q. 5,184.
[2] Second Appendix to Fourth Report, Royal Commission on Civil Service (Cd. 7340 of 1914), Q. 22,591.
[3] *Ibid.*, pp. 49 and 105.
[4] First Appendix to Fourth Report, Royal Commission on Civil Service (Cd. 7339 of 1914), p. 23.

upon the market rates paid to men and women. " We did not fix the lower payment for women than men—we found it," he declared.[1]

It has not been easy in the past to tell how great is the money value set by the Government upon pension and sick leave privileges. If a definite attempt had been made to estimate their value we might expect to find unestablished servants receiving proportionately high salaries. In the branches in which temporary labour was most needed, however, the pressure of competition for employment has been so great as to bring the rate even lower than that for permanent work. The worker is quite ready to acknowledge the value of establishment privileges, and much testimony to their influence in making workers more or less contented was forthcoming in evidence tendered to the Royal Commission of 1914. One witness stated that " thoroughly qualified officials willingly accept secure, though moderate, prospects in lieu of more remunerative outside employment under conditions involving possible risk for the future."[2] Continuity and security are valuable assets and may be justly allotted a money value ; but if this is done, then workers engaged temporarily should receive compensation for the absence of such assurances. Of the principle having been applied in this way there is no evidence whatever.[3]

Fresh questions arise as soon as classification of officers, with their respective scales of salary, has

[1] Second Appendix to Fourth Report, Royal Commission on Civil Service (Cd. 7340 of 1914), Q. 31,395.

[2] First Appendix to Fourth Report, Royal Commission on Civil Service (Cd. 7339 of 1914), p. 10.

[3] Evidence before the Royal Commission in 1914 on this point is interesting.   Mr. E. Murphy (Irish Land Commission) stated that in his office there were 16 temporary clerks whose

been decided. Most of these questions are due to the very broad lines of recruitment and the numerous divisions of work which that method deliberately leaves out of account. The questions are less pressing and the difficulties less awkward, because of the isolation of the Service for which officers are secured by these means. Government employment of this kind stands practically alone. It is not—as the Commission in 1914 avowed—run as though it were a business.[1] It bears slight resemblance to any private enterprise, and the workers assert that private employers are never anxious to engage a clerk who has been trained in Government employment. Government Departments represent to a large degree monopoly undertakings, and the Civil Service an isolated set of professions. Thus the care necessary in securing employees does not extend to the retaining of them after the first few years. By that time they are fitted for Government work, and there is no large market for the labour they have to sell, outside Government Departments. These facts have meant in the past

services ranged from 23 years down to 11 years, and the highest salary paid to any officer of that class was £2 10s. The second division clerks were on the scale £70 to £300.— Second Appendix to Fourth Report, Royal Commission on Civil Service (Cd. 7340 of 1914), Q. 28,391.

The following extract from the cross-examination of Sir Bernard Mallet (Registrar-General) by Mr. Philip Snowden, is also significant : " I find the average paid to your temporary staff (women) is 12s. a week, £30 a year ? "—" Yes."—" If these women had been successful (in Civil Service examinations) and had received appointments in the Post Office, their salaries would not have been 18s. a week ; they would have begun at £65 a year ? "—" Yes."—Appendix to Second Report, Royal Commission on Civil Service (Cd. 6535 of 1914), Qs. 10,012 and 10,023.

[1] Fourth Report, Royal Commission on Civil Service (Cd. 7338 of 1914), par. 86.

that offices might be organized with very slight reference to the difficulty of the work concerned, or to the ability or energy required to perform it. Offices were " graded " in many instances by the Treasury. This has been literally true in the case of new offices ; and virtually true in relation to older departments as they expanded and their needs increased. All proposals for increasing the number of first or second division officers, or for adding to the staff of any office, must be submitted to the Treasury, and the sanction or veto of the Finance Department is final, unless Parliamentary pressure can be exerted. An example of the Treasury's deciding definitely upon the staffing of an office was laid before the Royal Commission by the Chairman of the National Health Insurance Commission for Wales. The Treasury had resolved that the office of that Insurance Commission should be an " intermediate " office, that is to say, that its principal posts should be filled by men of a sort of supplementary class who enter by an examination which is slightly better than that for the second division, but still considerably below the standard for the first division. There was perhaps some foundation for the excuse of the Treasury that it was nearly impossible to get first division men to go to Wales, but the result of bowing to this, instead of offering higher pay for work in uncongenial surroundings, was that some duties which the Insurance Commission thought should be placed in the hands of most highly qualified men was done by officers of lower status and at lower rates of pay.[1] The office of the Registrar-General in England was similarly graded by the

[1] Second Appendix to Fourth Report, Royal Commission on Civil Service (Cd. 7340 of 1914), pp. 84–9.

Treasury, and in 1895 the following ruling on the subject was issued by the Lords Commissioners of the Treasury : " It must be understood that My Lords cannot admit the existence in your Department at any time of an upper division in the present sense of the term, or that an establishment of staff officers and clerks of the second division are not to be regarded as equal to the discharge of all the duties of the office." [1]

Another case in which grading was apparently arbitrary is that of the two main sections of the Post Office administration. In the secretary's office employment was found for 59 first division officers before 1914, while in the accountant-general's office, there were none.[2] It would be difficult to prove that none of the accounts work of the Post Office was sufficiently important to require first division men. The economy idea is carried a step further in the Post Office. For the purpose of filling what may be called " staff posts " by men other than those of the first division, a new class called supplementary clerks was formed. These were recruited from Post Office servants who had not less than two years' service and were not older than 26. An examination, about equal to that for the second division, was set, and (with the above provisos) the appointments were competitive. This scheme produced two results of special note. One was that there remained in the Post Office no staff posts to which second division men might be promoted ; [3] the other was that the labour obtained was cheaper than it would have

---

[1] Appendix to Second Report, Royal Commission on Civil Service (Cd. 6535 of 1914), Q. 9,773.

[2] Second Appendix to Fourth Report, Royal Commission on Civil Service (Cd. 7340 of 1914), p. 343.

[3] *Ibid.*, p. 354.

been if senior second division men had been promoted. The salaries of second division clerks in 1914 were on a scale of £70 to £300. The supplementary clerks were divided into three grades with scales of £100 to £200, £200 to £300, and £300 to £400.[1] Only in the later years of a supplementary clerk's service (for promotion from grade to grade was contingent upon vacancies) would a salary above that of the ordinary second division be paid.

Promotion from the second to the first division has been quite uncommon. The best that a second division clerk could hope for was a staff clerkship at a salary which might rise to £450. He still remained a second division clerk, and promotion to the first division, even if he secured it, might be a prospective rather than an immediate improvement. The Vice-President of the L.G.B. for Ireland in 1913 told the Royal Commission, " You may have a staff clerk who would like to be promoted but cannot afford it, he loses so much money."[2] This is easily understood, for though the limit of the first division scale was £500 its starting point was £200 a year, and on promotion to the first division a second division clerk (who had risen to a staff post with special pay) might receive only (a) the minimum of the scale of the new post, or (b) the salary to which he would have been entitled as a second division clerk without the promotion to the staff post. On the other hand, a plain second division clerk, if promoted to the first division, might be granted the salary he would have received if he had entered the first division at the age

---

[1] Second Appendix to Fourth Report, Royal Commission on Civil Service (Cd. 7340 of 1914), p. 354.
[2] Ibid., Q. 27,241.

of 24 and received the normal increments of that class.[1] This type of penalization has not been confined to promotion. A raising of minimum salaries has occasionally produced a comparative hardship. An instance of this is found in the experience of surveyors and valuers on the staff of the Irish Land Commission. Up to 1894 their starting salary was £100. Then it was raised to £120, and new candidates entered the Service at the same salary as men who had served for two years and received their two increments of £10.[2] One assumes that in the judgment of the Treasury the value of the job has not increased, but merely that the market price at which the supply can be maintained has gone up. The old servants are bound by their handicap in the general market and by their desire not to lose Government privileges.

This principle has been carried still further in the matter of staff posts, to which in some offices it had become the custom to appoint second division clerks. It was complained by the second division clerks of the Irish Land Commission in 1913 that the Treasury had announced that the salaries of such posts were considered " personal " and were liable to revision in case of vacancy. The Secretary of the Land Commission asserted that this was merely a safeguard, and that there

[1] Appendix to Second Report, Royal Commission on Civil Service (Cd. 6535 of 1914), Qs. 10,896–7. Col. Sir E. W. D. Ward (Secretary to War Office) in his evidence said : " In 1903 we were desirous of promoting to the higher division two staff clerks, both of whom were in receipt of £380 a year. The effect of the Treasury condition was that these two gentlemen, who were competent in every respect to perform higher division work, would, as a consequence of such promotion, have had their pay reduced to £216 10s. and £240 respectively."

[2] Second Appendix to Fourth Report, Royal Commission on Civil Service (Cd. 7340 of 1914), p. 262.

was "nothing sinister about it" so far as his Department was concerned,[1] yet it does give support to the suspicion that advantage was being taken of the position of the employees to reduce the cost of administration.

Another rather mean modification was brought to light in 1914. The Class 1 men employed in the office of the L.G.B. in Ireland were paid on the scale £150, rising by £15 per annum to £300, and then by £20 increments to £500, though men of a similar grade employed at the English L.G.B. were on the ordinary scale of £200 by £20 to £500. The reply of the Treasury to a protest was " that living was so cheap in Ireland."[2] The low salaries of the higher ranks of officers in the Museum Service were also justified on the ground that there were exceptional opportunities for the pursuit of scientific and literary research in this branch.[3]

Not only was it possible thus to place first class work on second class men, but also the arbitrary grading of offices by the Treasury led to some confusion of duties. Assistant clerks, clamouring for higher pay, alleged that they frequently worked alongside second division clerks and did precisely similar work. Before the Royal Commission in 1914 the Vice-President of the Irish L.G.B. admitted that of much of the work it was "very hard to say to which class it belongs."[4] The lines of demarcation were bound to be blurred, while a veto on the requirements of an office was exercised by a distant authority.

[1] Second Appendix to Fourth Report, Royal Commission on Civil Service (Cd. 7340 of 1914), p. 306.

[2] *Ibid.*, p. 201.

[3] Fourth Report, Royal Commission on Civil Service (Cd. 7338 of 1914), par. 43.

[4] Second Appendix to Fourth Report, Royal Commission on Civil Service (Cd. 7340 of 1914), Q. 27,271.

Apparently the most valuable attribute of the higher division man was not the work he customarily carried out but his potential capacity for dealing with new work and overcoming fresh difficulties. An interesting comparison of the two divisions was laid before the Royal Commission by Mr. A. H. Norway (Secretary of the Dublin G.P.O.). Here are his views : " A second division clerk, choosing the most favourable specimen of his class, would be a man of great accuracy and great industry. He could be trusted implicitly to work without making grave errors, but he would be conspicuously inferior in the power of thinking out new situations, such as occur constantly in the public service now that the work becomes more complicated. The business of a first division man I take to be to find his way across uncharted seas. The second division man would not normally have acquired the powers of mind which would enable him to do that. He would not have the quality of insight or vision which comes from high education. He would not have the same power of balancing risks and probabilities, or of discovering the exact line of possibilities." [1]

The definite charge of speeding up was also made. The Irish land valuers declared in 1913 that their work had been increased by one hour per day as the result of the Finance Act of 1912, though they received no extra pay. It was contended then that their lodging allowance of 13s. 6d. a day represented a certain profit, and that their longer periods of absence from home on account of Finance Act work would in effect produce an increase in their incomes.[2]

[1] Second Appendix to Fourth Report, Royal Commission on Civil Service (Cd. 7340 of 1914), Q. 31,699.
[2] Ibid., p. 265.

The assistant clerks, whose market value was low, appear to have been treated least kindly of all. Some of the evidence given in 1913 conveyed the impression that they were actually a parasitic class in their earlier years of service. Their scale was £45 by £5 increments to £70, and then by £10 to £150. An official of the Irish Land Commission stated that many of the Irish assistant clerks who had gone to London applied for a transfer to Dublin, not because the cost of living was much lower, but because they would be able to live in Dublin with their parents or friends.[1]

The real abuse of monopoly power emerges from the story of unestablished labour. In 1914 there were 25,000 unestablished servants in the 80 Civil Service departments. The Post Office employed 122,000 persons who were not on the establishment, but a very small number of these were civil servants in the accepted sense.[2] The general tests by which the Government claims to regulate establishment are, whether the work in question is likely to form the lifework of the employee, or whether it will unfit him for competition in the general labour market.[3] Both tests in practice have proved extremely elastic, and

[1] Second Appendix to Fourth Report, Royal Commission on Civil Service (Cd. 7340 of 1914), Qs. 30,158-9.

[2] Fourth Report, Royal Commission on Civil Service (Cd. 7338 of 1914), pars. 4 and 5.

[3] Report, Hobhouse Committee on Post Office (H.C. 266 of 1907), par. 572, contains the following : " The Department stated that men were put on the establishment in cases where the employment was of such a character as to make it the lifework of an employee, but that where work was of a kind common to many employers, or temporary, or probationary, it was held to be of unestablishable character." Par. 601 adds : " The reason for not establishing factory hands was the fact that their labour had an outside marketable value."

some employments which were not intended to form a life's work have lengthened to individual service of as much as twenty years.[1] The majority of such workers were classed as " temporary clerks." " Temporary " was nearly always a wrong description. Clerks were attracted to such posts by the traditional security of Government employment, and they clung to them in the enduring hope that some day their claims to establishment would be admitted. The Royal Commission of 1914 selected Ireland as the home of the greatest part of this trouble. In Dublin alone there were said to be between 400 and 500 temporary clerks, none of whom received more than £2 10s. per week. [2] The Commission urged that special safeguards against excessive use of temporary labour were necessary, and described temporary clerical employment in Ireland as an " outstanding and demoralizing feature of departmental organization." [3]

The nearest approach to a parallel in England existed in the staffs of the solicitors to the Treasury, Board of Trade, and Works Loan Board. Here the Government had adopted the principle of giving to the heads of these sections a lump sum annually with which to pay for the labour they required. There appear to have been two genuine reasons for choosing

[1] First Appendix to Fourth Report, Royal Commission on Civil Service (Cd. 7339 of 1914), p. 10 ; and Second Appendix to Fourth Report, Royal Commission on Civil Service (Cd. 7340 of 1914), Q. 31,046 : " In the Registry of Deeds Department there are men who have spent 40 years in one department continuously ; these are paid on the piecework system."
[2] Second Appendix to Fourth Report, Royal Commission on Civil Service (Cd. 7340 of 1914), Q. 28,393.
[3] Fourth Report, Royal Commission on Civil Service (Cd. 7338 of 1914), par. 79.

this method : it was felt that solicitors would desire to select the particular type of servant they needed, and it was assumed that young men of the legal professions would take advantage of this opportunity to get a couple of years' experience in Government work and then leave the offices for private practice. Actually such an ebb and flow never took place.[1] The staffs of these departmental solicitors remained, and gave generally long service to the Government without security or prospect of pension although the ordinary rule making retirement compulsory at 65 applied to these workers as much as to those on the establishment. Whole classes of non-artisan workers at various departments were unestablished. These included technical assistants, draughtsmen, and clerks at the Office of Works ; electricians and stokers at the British Museum ; viewers at the Royal Dockyard, Woolwich, and at the Royal Army Clothing Depart· ment.[2] In the engineer services of the War Office many draughtsmen, surveyors, and clerks, with 20 years' service or more, were still not on the established list in 1914.[3] One-third of the inspectors employed by the Board of Agriculture and Fisheries at this time were unestablished, the Treasury assumption being that the work was " of a fluctuating nature."[4] Of 67 draughtsmen in the barrack construction department

[1] Fourth Report, Royal Commission on Civil Service (Cd. 7338 of 1914), par. 12.

[2] Appendix to Second Report, Royal Commission on Civil Service (Cd. 6535 of 1914), Q. 6,737.

[3] Ibid., Qs. 6,708–19.

[4] Ibid., Qs. 8,416–7. Sir Thomas Elliott (Permanent Secretary of Board of Agriculture and Fisheries), asked if the tendency was for the work to become permanent, said : " I think so, but we have not been able as yet to convince the Treasury that that is so."

of the War Office only 8 were pensionable.[1]   All these examples point in the same direction.

The original intention of Government to select the best workers and treat them with care becomes progressively less pronounced as it is more clearly seen that the State service has no competitors for its labour.   The monopolist position engendered a series of high-handed alterations which affected the workers adversely and offered them no compensation.   The worst feature of all was the departure from the establishment theory to such an extent that by 1914 nearly 50 per cent. of the State's servants were unestablished. The system meant a saving in expense.   Generally no other reason was suspected by those who came into immediate touch with the workers.   The Permanent Secretary of the War Office told the Royal Commission that he knew of no reason why so many of his staff should be unestablished " except expense." [2] There is a similar tendency also in the retention of the old rule that candidates for posts in the Diplomatic Service must have a private income of at least £400 a year.[3]   This is a matter in which practically all European Governments have adopted the same policy, and is undoubtedly a Department in which the social accomplishments of candidates are important, but its conservative treatment to-day has the effect of placing the diplomatic branch outside the sphere of ordinary wage-negotiations and of saving the taxpayer some of the "overhead charges " of the Foreign Office business.[4]

In view of the method of recruiting and of Treasury control, it is not surprising that one seeks in vain for

[1] Appendix to Second Report, Royal Commission on Civil Service (Cd. 6535 of 1914), Q. 10,971.
[2] Ibid., Q. 10,978.   [3] Ibid., Q. 2,574
[4] This system has been recently abolished.

any correlation of remuneration to output or effort. The failure to attempt this is most noticeable in the treatment of the women problem. The Post Office confessed in 1914 that the reason for employing women in increasing proportion was economy.[1] The English National Health Insurance Commission, when it was set up, availed itself freely of female labour. The Board of Education, by 1914, was stated to have handed over some of the work formerly done by men to women.[2] In no case, however, prior to 1914 had any real attempt been made to arrive at a ratio which would apportion the wages of women according to the relation of their efficiency and output to that of men. In the matter of the Insurance Commission, Sir Francis Mowat's Committee fixed the wages for men but shirked the female labour question. The Treasury decided the rates by the rule that they should be " slightly lower than men's." [3] The Royal Commission of 1914 found it impossible to leave the matter at that, condemned the obvious fact that there had been no " general consideration of the problem," and the majority of the Commission added : " For instance, we find that highly qualified women inspectors receive, in many cases, salaries little more than one-half of those paid to men of similar grade employed in the same department. We therefore recommend that the Treasury . . . should institute a general inquiry with the object of removing inequalities of salary not based on differences in the efficiency of service." [4] The

[1] See p. 113.
[2] Second Appendix to Fourth Report, Royal Commission on Civil Service (Cd. 7340 of 1914), p. 161.
[3] Fourth Report, Royal Commission on Civil Service (Cd. 7338 of 1914), p. 73.
[4] *Ibid.*, par. 21.

minority attempted to justify the disparities by reference to the " family wage " of men, put forward the usual economy plea, and expressed the conviction that women would not continue to be employed if absolute equality of wages were insisted upon.[1]

The Post Office had to deal with the beginnings of this question as early as 1906, up to which time women had been employed indiscriminately upon savings bank work, which they shared with men.[2] Their sick leave was shown to average only four days a year more than that of men.[3] The quality of their work was not alleged to be poorer than that of men, yet there was a wide difference in the wages of the two sexes. When the point was raised the Controller of the Savings Bank Department believed he could settle the question " once and for all " by setting the women on one particular kind of work alone and giving all the rest to the men. With this idea the whole of the ledger work was allotted to women, much to their annoyance, and all the other work of the office was handed to the men.[4] Women's wages remained practically unchanged. Clearly no real effort had been made to deal with any of the phases of the women's question up to 1914.

The Treasury allocation of staffs produced a further instance of the failure to correlate pay and effort. A Treasury Regulation provided that 50 per cent. of the typists in any office might be graded as shorthand-typists at wages of 26s. to 30s. per week, while the remaining 50 per cent. were to be merely typists at

[1] Fourth Report, Royal Commission on Civil Service (Cd. 7338 of 1914), par. 22.
[2] First Appendix to Fourth Report, Royal Commission on Civil Service (Cd. 7339 of 1914), p. 16.
[3] *Ibid.*, p. 17.   [4] *Ibid.*, p. 16.

6

20s. to 26s. per week.[1] The system was denounced by the Royal Commission. It took no cognizance of the actual needs of an office. In some Departments most of the work was copying, and little or no short-hand was required. Such offices, nevertheless, had their full complement of shorthand-typists, while in other sections, where the need for shorthand was great, women paid at the lower rate might find the use of shorthand indispensable.

The question of overtime is also one upon which a strange principle arose. No officer in receipt of £350 a year or more was expected to apply for overtime payment no matter how much he worked. It was stated in 1914 that if he applied for it he would get it, but undoubtedly the unwritten law was an effective deterrent. In most other cases overtime rates were calculated according to the salary of the officer, but in no circumstances was an increase in the rate made. Temporary clerks also were paid on the same basis with the exception of copyists, who, engaged sometimes at £1 per week, received overtime at the piecework rate of 1½d. per folio of 72 words.[2]

One of the accepted traditions of labour value the Government absolutely disregarded. In the Irish L.G.B. service medical inspectors were paid at the same rate as general inspectors, no special allowance being made for the special qualifications of the medical men.[3] In the English L.G.B., too, the medical inspectors were not valued at a salary equal to that set upon similar officers in the employ of large munici-

---

[1] Fourth Report, Royal Commission on Civil Service (Cd. 7338 of 1914), p. 94.

[2] Second Appendix to Fourth Report, Royal Commission on Civil Service (Cd. 7340 of 1914), p. 337.

[3] *Ibid.*, Q. 27,429.

palities. Their scale of £500 to £800 in 1914 was said to be " considerably less " than the pay of the medical officer of health of a big city.[1]

Adult messengers were as a whole a class whose pay, while better than that of their equivalent grade in the Post Office, seems to have been decided chiefly by market rates. Most of them were army, navy, and police pensioners, who received 21s. a week, though a Treasury minute permitted 25 per cent. of the messengers in any office to receive wages of 24s. In some few exceptional cases messengers were established and such men were paid on a scale of £70 to £120.[2] One divergence from its usual rule placed the Treasury in a predicament from which it extricated itself by a surprising determination to avoid an anomaly. By some means the office of the Road Board was allowed to have one messenger at 30s. a week. When the Development Commission was formed it was housed in the same building as the Road Board. It also needed a messenger. And that messenger must needs occupy the same room as the messenger of the Road Board. In order that there might not be what the Vice-Chairman of the Development Commission called " an invidious distinction," the Treasury agreed that this messenger also should receive the 30s. wage.[3]

[1] Appendix to Second Report, Royal Commission on Civil Service (Cd. 6535 of 1914), Qs. 7,116–8. Sir Horace Munro (Permanent Secretary of the L.G.B.) said he did not think on the whole there was any difficulty in getting the men they wanted. " It may be that occasionally there is a particular man, whom we would like to get, who is not tempted by the salary we are in a position to offer."

[2] Fourth Report, Royal Commission on Civil Service (Cd. 7338 of 1914), par. 34.

[3] Second Appendix to Fourth Report, Royal Commission on Civil Service (Cd. 7340 of 1914), p. 112.

The cost of living seems to have entered very slightly into wage questions. In the Report of the Royal Commission the chief reference to it is to be found in a short reservation subscribed to by eight members. " We believe," they said, " that efficiency in clerical, as in other forms of labour, depends in part upon the food, housing, recreation, etc., made possible by the salary paid. For this reason we think that no fair inference can be drawn as to the efficiency of the two sexes from a comparison between the work of the existing women clerks and that of male clerks enjoying much larger salaries." [1] That was all ; yet it has a strong bearing on much that is connected with the breakdown of the establishment theory and the increase in the employment of temporary clerks.

In 1914 great efforts were being made to convince the Government of the evils of the boy-copyist system. Between 1897 and 1911 boy-copyists to the number of 14,500 were recruited of whom only 4,500 succeeded in obtaining assistant clerkships. [2] The remainder, at the age of 20, were turned adrift to swell the ranks of partially trained workers. This, of course, was a toll levied upon the potentialities of the nation's labour supply, just as the early service of the assistant clerks represented a drain upon the other industries of the country. The Treasury's outlook up to 1914 on these matters was as restricted as it was in the matter of allotting staffs to offices. There is some ground for believing that the Treasury maintained an obscure sort of ratio between the numbers of first and second division and assistant clerks which an office might have. What that proportion was it is not easy to

[1] Fourth Report, Royal Commission on Civil Service (Cd. 7338 of 1914), reservation 6, par. 3.
[2] Ibid., p. 28.

discover, but its effect in many offices was to render
divisions of work indistinct, and the relating of pay
to effort impossible. Yet in 1914 the Royal Commission
was still giving expression to the old formula : " It
is an accepted principle with all parties that the
Government should be a ' model employer.' " [1]

The interpretation which might be set upon the
" model employer " in the light of this evidence is
that wages shall be fixed on the supply and demand
basis, that the privilege of establishment shall be extended very cautiously—in fact not to more than half
of the workers, that no compensation shall be given
to workers in lieu of establishment, and that payment
shall be made for status and qualifications rather than
for work done.   No attempt was made to bargain with
the workers in their organized capacity.   The war was
to enable that step forward to be taken.   Up to 1914
recognition of unions of civil servants had been
determinedly refused.   Again the Treasury was the
deciding factor.   Below is given its refusal of one
application for " recognition "—that of the Association
of Second Division Clerks : " I am directed to state
that, in their Lordships' opinion, it would not be in
the public interest that this request should be granted.
My Lords do not believe that the existing regulation
places unnecessary difficulties in the way of bringing
to the notice of the responsible authorities any representations which the second division clerks may desire
to make.   On the other hand, it is essential to good
order and discipline that the second division clerks
should not be privileged to take action independently
of the heads of their departments.   Clerks of the
second division should bear in mind that although the

[1] Fourth Report, Royal Commission on Civil Service
(Cd. 7338 of 1914), par. 87.

second division is a body common to the Civil Service, this fact does not affect their position as officers of the Departments they serve." [1]   The " existing regulation " was that all communications should be submitted through departmental heads.   Originally even this degree of concerted action had been disallowed. The arrangement insisted on by the Treasury in this case tended only to split up clerks, who were recruited by a uniform system, into departmental groups for bargaining purposes.

All such objections were to break down under the sanction given to Whitley Councils.   For many years while they held good, wages alone depended upon the play of economic forces, and the good intention to respect the personality of the workers gradually weakened.   Two instances of wage-fixing in response to market conditions may be gathered from a comparison between the class of artificers employed at the Mint and the class of assistant clerks.   The Mint must necessarily have highly skilled workmen, and to obtain them it often had to pay full outside rates, without any deduction in respect of pension rights. [2]   The Master of the Mint was allowed a fairly wide discretion in this matter.   When the class of assistant clerks was formed in 1896 the Treasury fixed the scale at £45, rising by £5 a year to £85, and then, if a certificate of efficiency was obtained, by £7 10s. to £150.   As assistants might be engaged at the age of 17, a man would be at least 25 years old before he received £85, and at the age of 30 his salary would be only £122 10s. But there was never any shortage of clerks, and the scale remained, making marriage practically impossible

[1] Appendix to Second Report, Royal Commission on Civil Service (Cd. 6535 of 1914), Q. 2,719.

[2] *Ibid.*, Qs. 8,092–5.

until the worker was about 30. The "living wage," as has been seen, did not enter into Treasury considerations, and in this instance is found proof of how ineffective may be, on occasions, responsibility to the House of Commons for the exercise of the prerogative. The class of assistant clerks was formed in 1896 on the authority of a Treasury minute. Not until two years later was that minute backed by an Order in Council,[1] and not until 1911, when all Government wages came under discussion, were its provisions noticed in Parliament.

Never since the system of open competition was introduced has there been a shortage of candidates for any of the three main divisions. The attraction of Government service has proved so strong that educational establishments such as Clarks' College exist almost exclusively for the purpose of preparing candidates. Disillusion has awaited some of the successful entrants, as in the case of assistant clerks who left Dublin for service in London at £45 a year.[2] Nevertheless, most of them have had to stick to their posts, partly because there is a very small market for their services outside, and particularly because the Service offers security and the hope of a pension. Of the draughtsmen employed by the Board of Agriculture and Fisheries, at a scale of £80, rising by £5 to £150, with no prospects of promotion, Sir Thomas Elliott said in 1914 : " It is not a career worthy of a man of any ability, and some of these men unfortunately have got a certain amount of ability. They have come in here and have not got the courage to give it up."[3]

[1] Appendix to Second Report, Royal Commission on Civil Service (Cd. 6535 of 1914), Qs. 2,959–62.

[2] See p. 76.

[3] Appendix to Second Report, Royal Commission on Civil Service (Cd. 6535 of 1914), Qs. 8,503–12.

Government service evidently does exercise an inordinate attraction. The wastage represented by the mass of unsuccessful candidates is incalculable. The immurement of talent in unstimulating conditions constitutes an absolute loss to the nation. The establishment system has partially broken down—chiefly in the lower ranks, where the heavy supply has rendered labour most cheap. It is largely the routine workers who have suffered—those whose work is practically mechanical, those who can perform only the type of work which thousands of others are capable of doing, those, in short, whose ability does not provide an incentive to conservation on the part of the employer. Out of this fact arises the suspicion that establishment in its early days was primarily a device for maintaining a stable and efficient staff, and that the humanitarian aspect has attached itself to it. It is undoubtedly true to-day that in the lower ranks of the Civil Service pension prospects are not indispensable in the interests of the Service. The personnel may be changed without dislocation and the supply is never short. Pension arrangements have suffered accordingly, and perhaps may be regarded as reflecting the increased supply of low grade clerical labour while actual money wages remained unchanged. Yet instability does not appear to have resulted. Many unestablished servants have held their posts for long periods and have given faithful service. Their claim to establishment is often as good as that of workers who are pensionable. The mere possibility of establishment ties them to their post, and it is clear that the Government has taken advantage of this hope and of its semi-monopolist position to secure labour without any concern for the labourer.

CHAPTER IV

THE POST OFFICE

THE Post Office is so completely an industry in itself that there is no private enterprise with which its conditions may be compared. It is evident that the Department could have little direct help from outside in the fixing of its wages. It has been compelled to make its own standards, and might conceivably have employed some ingenuity in arriving at them. As a business undertaking it was unique. Much of its work was new, and should at least have been assessed according to some definite scheme. Most of the acknowledged business methods were inapplicable. It was practically impossible, for instance, to show a profit and loss account, since a large part of the Post Office income is revenue derived from taxation. Nor could a fair balance-sheet have been produced if this difficulty had not existed, for political considerations have occasionally been allowed to influence postal arrangements along lines which business considerations alone could never have admitted.[1] Owing also to the method of keeping accounts no reliable estimate has been possible as to

[1] Mr. Austen Chamberlain, when Postmaster-General in 1903, stated that the Imperial Penny Post was not intended to be remunerative, but was established " to promote facilities for the cultivation of closer relations with our fellow-subjects beyond the seas."—" Hansard," May 11, 1903.

the profitableness of the telegraphic as compared with the postal side of the undertaking. In 1903 it was privately calculated that there had been a loss of a million pounds on the telegraphs in the preceding year,[1] yet the average annual surplus derived from the Post Office rose from £3,728,800 during the years 1897–1902 to £4,473,400 in the period 1902–1907.[2] In deciding upon wages, therefore, the Department could not apply the ordinary business tests of profit and loss, or single out as profitable any particular branch. It was compelled to regard its work chiefly as a national service, and opposition has naturally been offered throughout to every effort to consider the surplus in relation to wage questions. At the same time comparisons with outside labour of types similar to those employed by the Post Office could not be made.[3] Further, wage questions in the Department might not easily be settled by the normal industrial method. If bargaining failed, the possibility of resort to a strike was extremely remote. The Secretary of the Post Office, in 1906, admitted that the strike was not " a method readily available to Government servants."[4]

By what methods then have the wage-rates been decided ? The Hobhouse Committee in 1907 came to

[1] Estimate by Mr. Henniker Heaton, who complained that in the year in question, although only ninety million telegrams had been sent, three hundred million forms had been used.— " Hansard," June 8, 1903.

[2] Mr. Asquith, Budget statement.—" Hansard," May 8, 1906.

[3] Report, Holt Committee on Post Office (H.C. 268 of 1913), par. 14 : " Your Committee find it extremely difficult to compare the conditions of Post Office service with those in any outside employment."

[4] Evidence, Hobhouse Committee on Post Office (H.C. 380 of 1907), Q. 181.

the conclusion that some of the salaries had been "fixed arbitrarily," [1] but no such admission has ever been made by the Department when workers have been pressing for higher pay. Postmen were given to understand that at least seven items were considered in fixing rates. These were, cost of living, labour values in particular localities, regard to " what it was found necessary to pay," consideration for the nature of the work, allowance for the element of trust, and the value of Christmas boxes. [2] An additional point was put forward by the Department in defence of its system of dividing London into three zones for the purpose of postmen's wages. Higher rates were allotted to the men working in the city, it was said, to allow for the expense of travelling, and for the extra time spent by the officers in getting to their work. [3] The real test which the Post Office applied to wage questions generally was stated by the Secretary of the Post Office in 1906. He did not admit the arbitrariness of the early standards, but he seemed to feel that wages grew up in somewhat haphazard fashion, and that, having arrived, they might be tested by experiment. The facts that the Service commanded a sufficient supply of candidates and that the quality of the candidates was good, he advanced as justification of the rates paid. [4] This simply means that the Department sought to set such

[1] Report, Hobhouse Committee on Post Office (H.C. 266 of 1907), par. 548.
[2] Evidence, Stanley Committee on Post Office (Cd. 2171 of 1904), pp. 142–3.
[3] Report, Hobhouse Committee on Post Office (H.C. 266 of 1907), par. 330.
[4] *Ibid.*, Qs. 181 and 185. Mr. H. Babington Smith said : " There are two tests which, I think, are applicable there as well as in private employment—in the first place, the test of

rates as were needed to secure the necessary labour without being challenged to justify its decisions. On this interpretation the basis was purely one of supply and demand. Even without this avowal, evidence is available which leads to the same conclusion. Scales of pay have, occasionally, had to be amended owing to shortage of supply. During the Boer War candidates were few, and at Manchester, Sheffield, and Birmingham the initial wages for sorting clerks and telegraphists had to be raised from 12s. to 16s. per week.[1] Similarly, the attractions of Post Office employment were not sufficient to deter employees from accepting engagements with cable companies and in colonial telegraph services when the opportunity occurred during 1901–1903. From the Glasgow office alone, in these years, 110 telegraphists resigned.[2] Evidently the Post Office, despite its special advantages, was offering wages so near the market level that competition for its workers was easily possible. The basic principle, however, was quite bluntly admitted in 1906, when it was complained that the pay of clerks working the post offices on board Atlantic mail-boats, was less than half that of the American clerks working on the same boats. The Department justified its contention that the pay was sufficient on the ground that there was "great competition for these appointments."[3] As long ago as 1891 the Postmaster of

whether the wages command a sufficient supply of candidates. . . . The second point in which the same considerations can be applied in Government service as in private service is as regards the qualifications of persons entering the service."

[1] Evidence, Stanley Committee on Post Office (Cd. 2171 of 1904), pp. 84 and 132.

[2] Ibid., p. 87.

[3] Report, Hobhouse Committee on Post Office (H.C. 266 of 1907), pars. 291–2.

Leeds feared he would have to raise the wages of boy telegraph messengers from 5s. to 6s. because of the competition of mills and factories in the city for boy labour.[1]

It is clear what the basis of these wages really was. Yet development brought two subordinate principles, which were devoted to the working out of details after the broad lines had been laid down. These were an attempt to secure a relationship between wages and output, and a tendency at the same time to rate workers rather than jobs. The two at first glance seem contradictory, and only the fact that the scheme which aimed at payment by results was of a very half-hearted type made it possible for them to exist together. Had the former of these approached success the other could not have remained at its side.

The new system has been in operation since 1897, when first the Post Office tried to make distinctions between the relative value of work done by bodies of men of the same grade. The distinctions were confined to bodies of workers and were not carried as far as individuals. Hence its failure either to produce payment by results or to leave wholly intact the idea of payment according to status. Under this scheme the work of post offices throughout the country was rendered in terms of a single unit. Every type of work was expressed in terms of letters dealt with, a postal order or telegram being reckoned as so many letters. By this test the volume of work at the various offices was judged, and the offices divided into six classes, each with different scales of pay for the indoor staff.[2] This, it was assumed, would provide

[1] Evidence (unpublished), Raikes Inquiry on Post Office (1891), Q. 1,851.

[2] Report, Hobhouse Committee on Post Office (H.C. 266 of 1907), par. 256.

a reliable indication of the pressure under which work would have to be done, and of the need for extra remuneration to cover the special effort necessary to work at high speed. No preliminary investigation as to the uniform distribution of staff at the various offices appears to have been made, and it does not seem to have occurred to the Department that in seeking to base wages on work done it should first have made sure that the existing allocation of staff (and therefore of aggregate expenditure on wages in each office) to work was regular. Once set up the unit test was vigorously defended by the Department. Even when confronted by what looked like anomalies, departmental officials claimed that an office in a comparatively small town, like Taunton, which acted as a forwarding centre and therefore had a high proportion of night-work was justly placed on a higher scale than a bigger town which performed no such work.[1] This contention is remarkable since it implies extra allowance, under two headings, in respect of night-work, which was ordinarily paid for on the special basis of counting seven hours' work as eight between the hours of 10 p.m. and 6 a.m.

A similar method was in use also for fixing the salaries of postmasters and the remuneration of sub-postmasters. In the case of postmasters the Department confessed that the "unit" scale was unsatisfactory in that it awarded an excessive value to "forward" work.[2] In 1907 no fewer than 21,601 sub-postmasters were paid (on a commission basis which involved consideration of some 70 different

[1] Evidence, Stanley Committee on Post Office (Cd. 2171 of 1904), pp. 189–90.
[2] Report, Hobhouse Committee on Post Office (H.C. 266 of 1907), par. 548.

items grouped under 24 heads) sums varying from £7 10s. to about £1,000 a year.[1] This certainly approached more nearly to payment by results, though it provided no means of adjusting payment to new methods. For example, the poundage on stamps sold remained the same when the cost of postage was reduced, and the increase in the number of stamps sold caused more work, with a smaller return. Again, there was a decrease in the commission on postal orders presented in bulk by banks, though it was necessary to make a separate entry of each order.

This, however, was more a matter of adjustment than of principle. The important item was that affecting salaried workers, who were paid according to two standards. The class of sorting clerk and telegraphist was common to the whole of the United Kingdom outside London. Theoretically, every officer of similar rank was capable of performing the work of his class and might be transferred if necessity demanded it to any office in the country. As a sorting clerk and telegraphist he was allotted a definite valuation by the Department, but such valuation depended upon the volume of work done by the office at which he was required to work. Underlying the system is a confusion of volume and quality.

The distinction was very broad, and within its wide limits what really mattered was the status of an officer. Upon that, rather than upon the work which he actually did in a given period, depended his pay, holidays, emoluments, and ultimate pension. With incremental scales it is difficult to see how this can be avoided, but the rigid application of the rule has

---

[1] Report, Hobhouse Committee on Post Office (H.C. 266 of 1907), pars. 508-17.

produced curious results. A London sorter in 1907 stated that he was receiving higher wages than other sorters of equal service in the sorting department because he had entered the sorters' class from another grade.[1] Except for the night-work allowance and the rule that Sunday duty be paid for at the rate of time and a half, the last vestige of payment for work done vanished in 1897, when the Tweedmouth Committee abolished extra payments to sorters for dealing with foreign mails and registered letters.[2] The mass rule had an interesting sequel when female clerical labour was admitted to the Post Office to undertake work which had previously been done jointly by men and boys. The second division male clerk entered the Service at £70 a year; the boy clerk received about £39. The new women clerks got £55.[3] Until 1913 officers who did the work of absent superiors received no extra pay, and were sometimes worse off than they would have been if they had remained at their own work.[4] The Department was officially cognizant only of the rank and grade of an employee, and could take no account of the nature of his individual service.

Beside these systems must be set the contention that the Post Office, in its strong position as monopolist, has used its advantage to secure labour at a cheap price. This was the charge brought by the workers who, from 1890, fought for a "living wage."[5] Just

[1] Evidence, Hobhouse Committee on Post Office (H.C. 380 of 1907), Qs. 1,891–2.
[2] Evidence, Stanley Committee on Post Office (Cd. 2171 of 1904), p. 53.
[3] Evidence, Hobhouse Committee on Post Office (H.C. 380 of 1907), pp. 979–80.
[4] See pp. 110–11.
[5] Evidence, Stanley Committee on Post Office (Cd. 2171 of 1904), Q. 944.

as it is difficult, owing to the absence of analogous
conditions in private employment, to find outside
standards with which to compare Post Office wages,
so it has been extremely difficult for a Post Office
servant to find employment for which he is fitted
outside the Department. That was urged as the
reason why postal servants consented to work for
wages rising from 12s. by slow increments to 34s. per
week in the case of provincial sorting clerks and
telegraphists,[1] and from 12s. to 20s. in the case of
rural postmen.[2] It is certain, at all events, that
economy was a strong influence in wage matters, and
some of the grievances ventilated by the workers were
possible only because of the monopoly element and
of the absence of trade union recognition. Until 1907
no determined effort had been made by the Department
to ensure an equality of real wages. The volume of
work unit was attacked by the workers in 1903, when
it was suggested that the cost of living was of more
importance. The Department met this with an
argument which suggested that the " unit " schedule
operated with a sort of accidental justice all round.
An official declared that " generally speaking " the
maximum pay of the various classes varied according
to the cost of living in different districts because, in
a rapidly growing industrial centre or residential
town, " the expansion of trade and growth of population which enhanced the cost of living also increased
the volume of Post Office work." [3] How far this
view was justified may be gathered from the table
on page 98. In very few cases was there coincidence

[1] Evidence, Stanley Committee on Post Office (Cd. 2171
of 1904), Q. 135.
[2] *Ibid.*, p. 157.   [3] *Ibid.*, p. 184.

7

between the Department's schedule figure, when expressed in terms of an index, and the corresponding

REAL WAGES, 1907.[1]

Male Sorting Clerks and Telegraphists.

Office	Min.	Max.	Mean	Wage Index	Cost of Living Index	Disparity in Percentages
	s. d.	s. d.	s. d.			
London	18 0	62 0	40 0	100	100	Nil
Manchester ..	12 0	56 0	34 0	85	86	— 1
Birmingham ..	12 0	56 0	34 0	85	85	Nil
Liverpool	12 0	56 0	34 0	85	86	— 1
Leeds	12 0	54 0	33 0	82·5	86	— 3·5
Cardiff	12 0	54 0	33 0	82·5	91	— 8·5
Derby	12 0	52 0	32 0	80	85	— 5
Gloucester.. ..	12 0	52 0	32 0	80	83	— 3
Swansea	12 0	52 0	32 0	80	90	—10
Blackburn.. ..	12 0	48 0	30 0	75	81	— 6
Wigan	12 0	48 0	30 0	75	80	— 5
Woolwich[2] ..	12 0	48 0	30 0	75	94	—19
Macclesfield ..	12 0	44 0	28 0	70	78	— 8
St. Helens ..	12 0	44 0	28 0	70	84	—14
Merthyr Tydvil ..	12 0	40 0	26 0	65	88	—23
Kidderminster ..	12 0	40 0	26 0	65	83	—18
Castleford ..	12 0	38 0	25 0	62·5	86	—23·5
Sheerness	12 0	38 0	25 0	62·5	95	—32·5
Edinburgh ..	12 0	56 0	34 0	100	100	Nil
Aberdeen ..	12 0	52 0	32 0	94·1	94	·1
Perth	12 0	48 0	30 0	88	98	—10
Dublin	12 0	56 0	34 0	100	100	Nil
Belfast	12 0	54 0	33 0	97	101	— 4
Cork	12 0	52 0	32 0	94·1	89	5·1
Limerick	12 0	48 0	30 0	88	91	— 3

[1] Wage figures, for this table and the succeeding one, are taken from the Appendices and Minutes, Report, Hobhouse Committee (H.C. 380 of 1907), p. 36 *et seq.* ; and the cost of living indices from the Board of Trade report on Cost of Living (Cd.3864 of 1908).

[2] For Woolwich, the Board of Trade rent index was 88. The cost of living figure is obtained by assuming retail prices to be general for the Metropolitan area at 100, and striking an average which is rough, but which errs on the right side.

index figure of the cost of living for the town concerned. In no case in England did the wage-index exceed the cost of living figure, and a comparison of this sort emphasizes the anomalies which were early brought to the notice of the Department by the workers.[1]

It will be seen that the unit of work did not produce results corresponding to the difference in cost of living. The disparities shown in the above table are nearly all of the " minus " type. In other words real wages were not maintained by this device.

Postmen's wages were fixed by different methods[2] and with fewer resultant shortcomings, as the table on page 100 shows.

By 1907 the Department was asking the Board of Trade for help as to the cost of living, but its conversion had been a slow process. In 1898, when the staff of the Brighton office complained of high expenses and the consequent reduction of their real wages the Department replied that " the incomes of the officers could be increased by the letting of apartments," [3] an attitude similar to that which held that a rural postman might be paid a poor wage because he would have three or four hours at the extreme point of his journey in which he could do other work such as boot-repairing or gardening.[4] Thus for many years cost of living did not enter into the wage calculations.

Some thought, however, had apparently been given to the fixing of maintenance wages. This is evident from the very small margin separating the minimum

[1] See p. 109.
[2] *Supra*, p. 99.
[3] Evidence, Stanley Committee on Post Office (Cd. 2171 of 1904), p. 97.
[4] See Appendix B.

wages for men and for women in most branches. As the scales rose the disparity became considerable, owing, as the Secretary of the Post Office said, in 1906,

Postmen

Office	Min.	Max.	Mean.	Wage Index	Cost of Living Index	Disparity in Percentages
	s. d.	s. d.	s. d.			
London (Div. 2) ..	19 0	32 0	25 6	100	100	Nil
Manchester ..	19 0	30 0	24 6	97·6	86	11·6
Birmingham ..	19 0	30 0	24 6	97·6	85	12·6
Liverpool	19 0	30 0	24 6	97·6	86	11·6
Leeds	19 0	28 0	23 6	92·2	86	6·2
Cardiff	19 0	28 0	23 6	92·2	91	1·2
Derby	19 0	28 0	23 6	92·2	85	7·2
Gloucester.. ..	18 0	24 0	21 0	82·3	83	− ·7
Swansea	18 0	26 0	22 0	86·5	90	− 3·5
Blackburn.. ..	18 0	26 0	22 0	86·5	81	5·5
Wigan	18 0	26 0	22 0	86·5	80	6·5
Woolwich	19 0	28 0	23 6	92·2	94	− 1·8
Macclesfield ..	18 0	24 0	21 0	82·3	78	4·3
St. Helens ..	18 0	26 0	22 0	86·5	84	2·5
Merthyr Tydvil ..	18 0	24 0	21 0	82·3	88	− 5·7
Kidderminster ..	18 0	24 0	21 0	82·3	83	− ·7
Castleford ..	18 0	24 0	21 0	82·3	86	− 3·7
Sheerness	18 0	22 0	20 0	79·6	95	−15·4
Edinburgh ..	19 0	30 0	24 6	100	100	Nil
Aberdeen	18 0	26 0	22 0	89·8	94	− 4·2
Perth	18 0	24 0	21 0	85·7	98	−12·3
Dublin	19 0	30 0	24 6	100	100	Nil
Belfast	19 0	28 0	23 6	95·9	101	− 5·1
Cork	18 0	26 0	22 0	89·8	89	·8
Limerick	18 0	24 0	21 0	85·7	91	− 5·3

to the fact that " the current value of male labour " was undoubtedly higher than that of female labour.[1] The Department also seemed to have looked at the question of maintenance for postmen employed in the central zone of London, for it provided, even before

[1] Evidence, Hobhouse Committee on Post Office (H.C. 380 of 1907), Q. 304.

the era of Select Committees, that the starting wage of 18s. should rise to 20s. when the postman reached the age of 19 years.[1] For the other zones no similar allowance was made, and it is clear that while some regard was had to the subsistence level, no thorough effort was made to arrive at a " living wage." Any such attempt would have called forth numerous examples of workers who could not live decently on the wages paid. One case laid before the Stanley Committee in 1903 may be quoted. " At the West Central District Office," said a witness, " a man with 21s. 6d. wages, whose rent and travelling is 11s. 6d. weekly with a wife and two children to support, has 8s. 6d. left with which to buy food, clothing, and fuel for four persons. It is interesting to observe that this is about the sum which is spent on one London pauper."[2]

The " current wage " was a much more effective influence than the living wage. During the early years of this century the habit of collecting statistics as to wages in various localities had been adopted by the Post Office. Such figures were collected in Ireland,[3] and when the help of the the President of the Board of Trade was invoked, special request was made that account should be taken of " wages paid in the localities generally."[4] In 1905 the Postmaster-General (Lord Stanley) himself proposed for rural postmen a lower rate than had been recommended

[1] Evidence, Stanley Committee on Post Office (Cd. 2171 of 1904), p. 161.
[2] *Ibid.*
[3] Evidence, Hobhouse Committee on Post Office (H.C. 380 of 1907), Q. 9,917.
[4] *Ibid.* Q. 7,215. Mr. A. Wilson Fox (Board of Trade) quoted letters from the Post Office to the Board of Trade, *re* cost of living inquiry.

by his Select Committee, where " the current rate of wages is exceptionally low." [1]　In all these movements the intention of the Department was apparently to arrange that its rates should be sufficiently high to attract the types of labour it required, but should not exceed that, at least until some years of service had merited a reward.

It is when the labour supply has been secured, and workers committed to a service which has no corresponding enterprise outside, that the element of monopolist autocracy is seen. In all grades the minima have been low and the increments small. Usually from 19 to 22 years were necessary to reach a maximum. A sorter, with 12 years' service, was receiving in 1903 only £110.[2] The minimum of the scale for sorting clerks and telegraphists at the same time was 12s. a week, which was paid to all— male and female—on appointment, after an indefinite period of service as a learner at 5s. or 6s. a week. The view of the Department as to the sufficiency of this wage, with its very small yearly increments, in the case of women workers, may be seen in the Post Office regulation that all women officers must live with their parents or guardians, or with some friend of whom the parent or guardian approved.[3] This was partly aimed, of course, at safeguarding the respectability of the women officers, but its bearing on the wage question is obvious.

The " apprentice " period for this class was even

[1] Memorandum by Postmaster-General on the Report of the Stanley Committee, issued March 24, 1905.

[2] Evidence, Stanley Committee on Post Office (Cd. 2171 of 1904), Qs. 401–3.

[3] Report, Hobhouse Committee on Post Office (H.C. 266 of 1907), par. 231.

less satisfactory. The Department tried to recruit learners only in such numbers as would be needed to fill vacancies after a reasonable period of instruction. Its estimates of probable vacancies were sometimes so far from the actual events that learners remained unappointed for periods varying from 9 months to 5 years 9 months.[1] The reply of Lord Stanley, in 1904, to the specific charge that five learners at Leeds had been employed for 2½ years at 5s. per week, with brief intervals of substitution duty, was that " this was due to the fact that the telegraph work at Leeds had not increased so rapidly as was expected."[2] It is true that there was no legal breach of contract in failing to give learners full-grade work within a reasonable time, but candidates, who were selected by open competition and who attained efficiency during training, certainly had a moral right to expect employment in the service for which they had been invited to compete.

When appointed, a sorting clerk and telegraphist's pay was low, if judged not merely by the standard of subsistence wages, but in comparison with the pay of other grades in Government service. Workers in 1903 contrasted this minimum of 12s. per week with the wage of a boy copyist in the Civil Service, which was 15s., and with the starting salary of a " lower division " clerk (£1 6s. 10d.)[3] and pointed to

[1] Evidence, Stanley Committee on Post Office (Cd. 2171 of 1904), p. 101. Miss Muriel Slade (a sorting clerk and telegraphist) quoted the case of a learner at Leicester, who remained unappointed for 5 years 9 months, doing substitution duty when necessary at 10s. to 15s. a week, and reverting to the school rate of 5s. when the staff was complete. She mentioned other cases of unappointed service of from 9 months to 2½ years.

[2] " Hansard," April 25, 1904.

[3] Evidence, Stanley Committee on Post Office (Cd. 2171 of 1904), p. 114.

the extraordinary situations which sometimes arose from the departmental rule, which made a sorting clerk and telegraphist liable to refund any money losses incurred while on counter duty. An officer of two years' service laid the following statement before the Stanley Committee in 1903 : " The total number of errors, for all kinds of work, recorded against me is only seven, so that I am not altogether careless. While receiving only 14s. a week wages, on each of two occasions I lost 20s." [1] Labour of this type might be justly described as cheap, and further support of the determination of the Department to pay no more than was necessary appears in the pay given to pensioned police officers. A notable case was that of lobby officers and cloak-room attendants, who were originally recruited from the class of tube attendants, and paid at the rate of 40s. per week. With the reservation of these posts for pensioned police officers the rate of pay fell to 22s.[2] In such cases a general Treasury rule demands a reduction in pay of " not less than 10 per cent."[3] But the Post Office had reduced the wages for this grade by about 45 per cent., despite the admission that ex-police officers could perform the duty more efficiently than the class of men from which it had been taken.[4]

[1] Evidence, Stanley Committee on Post Office (Cd. 2171 of 1904), p. 132.

[2] Evidence, Hobhouse Committee on Post Office (H.C. 380 of 1907), Qs. 10,532–45.

[3] Appendix to Second Report, Royal Commission on Civil Service (Cd. 6535 of 1914), Q. 11,481.

[4] Evidence, Hobhouse Committee on Post Office (H.C. 380 of 1907), Q. 10,778. Mr. A. F. King (Second Secretary to Post Office), challenged on this point, said : " We did as an ordinary business house would do, I think ; we found the work could be equally well done, if not better done, by other people and much cheaper."

Where possible, therefore, rate-cutting has actually taken place. The other aspect of cutting—speeding up—is much more difficult to detect, and may depend upon such a variety of causes that it may not be readily discerned. New instruments for telegraphists, additional regulations for counter clerks, building operations on a postman's " walk," may or may not have added to the intensity of the workers' efforts. Only in regard to telephone operators has a charge been definitely formulated. On this subject the Holt Committee reported in 1914 as follows : " Complaint was made of the system of speeding up in particular, by comparing and posting up the average answering time of teams of operators and reprimanding operators in each team with the lowest total of calls." [1] The Committee was assured by the Department that " competition between groups of operators " was discouraged and " forbidden by the rules," [2] yet the Committee thought the charge sufficiently well-founded to deserve mention and condemnation.

Saving has also been effected in another and much wider sphere. Cheeseparing of the kind mentioned above is of slight importance in comparison with the economy resulting from a partial abandonment of the " establishment " system. It is commonly assumed that employees of the Post Office are specially favoured among the working classes, because they have certain privileges—sick pay, holidays, and pensions. The justice of that assumption may be gauged from the fact that of the 240,000 workers employed by the Post Office in 1913 no fewer than

[1] Report, Holt Committee on Post Office (H.C. 268 of 1913), par. 492.
[2] *Ibid.*, p. 158.

122,000 were " unestablished." [1]   This, no doubt, has arisen partly because of the rapid expansion of the service, partly owing to a tight holding of the purse-strings by the Treasury ; but very largely in consequence of the Department's own policy of attempting to meet new needs with half-measures. Only one instance of definite limitation by the Treasury of the ratio of established to " hired " workers is discoverable, and this is embodied in a provision that not more than 62 per cent. of the Post Office linemen may be borne on the establishment.[2]   In respect of workers other than factory hands the Department had its own standards for regulating admission to establishment.   Where employment was likely to constitute an officer's life-work, establishment privileges were to be allowed.[3]   Failure to adhere to this standard was said, in 1913, to have resulted from the discovery by postmasters and surveyors that they could meet expansion of work, without reorganizing duties, if they had recourse to unestablished labour.[4]   Among the unestablished grades there were assistant and auxiliary postmen, auxiliary sorters, adult night messengers, and assistants at head and sub-offices, besides such artisan and unskilled classes as could find a market for their labour outside the Post Office. Frequently such labour was by no means of a temporary character.   Evidence was given in 1906 that auxiliary sorters had been employed for twenty years

[1] Report (Fourth), Royal Commission on Civil Service (Cd. 7338 of 1914), pars. 4 and 5.
[2] Report, Hobhouse Committee on Post Office (H.C. 266 of 1907), par. 568.
[3] Ibid., p. 572.   Also see note on p. 76.
[4] Report, Holt Committee on Post Office (H.C. 268 of 1913), par. 118.

in the Inland Section of the Sorting Department at
the General Post Office, London.[1] Assistant postmen
are sometimes persons who, owing to age or physical
unfitness, are ineligible for establishment. More frequently they are probationary postmen who graduate
later into the established class. Auxiliary postmen
and sorters are usually part-time workers. Adult
night messengers were recommended for establishment by the Holt Committee in 1914. None of the
classes has shown records of sufficiently short service
to justify the description " temporary."

Since none of these workers shared in the benefits
of establishment, it might reasonably be expected that
their wages would be higher than those of established
workers of a similar grade. In fact the reverse was
the case. The pay of postmen generally in 1907
represented from 5d. to 6d. an hour, but the highest
scale for auxiliary postmen at that time was $4\frac{1}{2}$d.
an hour. Unless labour was short, 4d. an hour was
the highest rate usually paid.[2] The traditional
attraction of the Post Office Service has usually
produced a fair supply of labour, and higher rates
were infrequently paid. An unemployed person has
often accepted an auxiliary post and attempted to live
on the pay, though the Department would probably
have discharged him had it discovered that he had
no other means of support. The Department prefers
to utilize the spare time of such men as boot

[1] Evidence, Hobhouse Committee on Post Office (H.C. 380
of 1907), Q. 1,402.
[2] *Ibid.*, p. 559. Mr. G. H. Stuart, representing the Postmen's
Federation, made the following statement : " Surveyors are
specially instructed that not more than 4d. an hour shall be
paid, even where the scheme laid down by the Department
justifies $4\frac{1}{2}$d., unless it is impossible to get men at the lower
rate."

repairers, small tradesmen, small agriculturists, and Government messengers. It was admitted in 1907 that there were in Ireland 2,754 auxiliaries who had no other occupation besides that provided by the Post Office. When reminded that this situation admitted of a suspicion of sweating, the Secretary of the Post Office explained that " no other occupation" probably meant " living with their family and helping in working on a small farm, or otherwise assisting in the maintenance of the family." [1]

Here again, however, the significant point is that the labour was cheap. It is obviously impossible for the Department to avoid auxiliary labour at times of special pressure, but there seems no excuse for paying for it at less than the rate fixed for regular employment. One of the most serious allegations made in respect of this labour was laid before the Holt Committee in 1913. This Committee quoted a witness as saying " that casual labour was employed by the Post Office for the purpose of avoiding the rates recommended by the Hobhouse Committee, the rates for all unestablished labour being lower than for established." [2] The suggestion here is, that two or more auxiliaries were employed to do work which might have warranted the employment of a full-time established servant. A similar tendency to cut prices was visible in the treatment of manual workers. Telephone fitters, cable-jointers, pipe-laying hands and gang hands are all unestablished. In 1907 they were receiving wages which varied, for different grades, from 20s. to 38s. This worked out at less than the

<hr>

[1] Evidence, Hobhouse Committee on Post Office (H.C. 380 of 1907), Q. 10,143.

[2] Report, Holt Committee on Post Office (H.C. 268 of 1913), par. 118.

rate per hour secured to similar workmen by the fair wages clause of Government contracts.[1]

Unsatisfactory as these matters were to the workers, they were perhaps no more irritating than the anomalies produced by the " unit " system for indoor staff and the " zoning " system for London postmen. Under the volume of work schedules there was, in 1903, a difference of 8s. between the maxima of sorting clerks and telegraphists at Plymouth and at Devonport ; of 6s. between the maxima at Croydon and Woolwich ; of 20s. between the maxima at Manchester and Eccles, though, in each case, the places are contiguous or comparable as regards conditions.[2] Other disparities, equally indefensible, could be quoted, but these are sufficient to show what strange results the volume of work distinction could bring about. The " zoning " of London caused similar difficulties. Postmen who delivered letters on one side of Chelsea Bridge received different wages from those who delivered on the other, and the maximum wage of the postman who delivered letters at 234, Old Ford Road was 4s. less than that of the man who delivered at 232, Old Ford Road.[3] Clearly the " unit " system had no regard to cost of living, and in view of such disparities, it awarded an unreasonable value to high-speed work at a big office. As to the zones, the border-lines must inevitably produce anomalous conditions. The real grievance here was that until 1907 the zone boundaries had not been decided by any thorough examination of the conditions, and since the Board of Trade

[1] Evidence, Hobhouse Committee (H.C. 380 of 1907), Q. 20,145.
[2] Evidence, Stanley Committee on Post Office (Cd. 2171 of 1904), pp. 101 and 165.
[3] *Ibid.*, p. 160.

investigation the zones have been revised, and in that form are still retained and operate probably with a large degree of justice.

Another matter in which the workers found themselves at a disadvantage was that of " substitution." The Department's system was condemned in 1914 by the Holt Committee. Prior to that time officers acted as substitutes for absent superiors, without receiving any extra pay, and sometimes actually lost on the change.[1] If substitution duty exceeded a period of six months, the substituting officer was entitled to receive superior pay for the duty in excess of that period. Evidence was produced, however, of certain instances in which men were kept at substitution work for five and a half months, then relieved for a fortnight, and returned to the substitution duty for another five and a half months.[2] The excuses for the system, offered by the Department, were that only by these means could holidays be arranged, and that such occasions gave a junior officer his chance of proving himself worthy of promotion.[3]   To this extent only has the scheme been countenanced by impartial

---

[1] Evidence, Stanley Committee on Post Office (Cd. 2171 of 1904), p. 165.   Mr. H. Urmston, a sorting clerk and telegraphist said : " In a case at Ormskirk, two bank holidays occurred during the postmaster's leave and the sorting clerk and telegraphist acting for the postmaster received no extra pay or days off. Had he been performing his own duty he would have received 5¼ hours' pay for both bank holidays, and he loses 8s. 6d. each Sunday when acting for the postmaster."

[2] *Ibid.*, p. 129; and Evidence, Hobhouse Committee (H.C. 380 of 1907), Qs. 6,363–5.   Before the latter Committee the Postmaster and Surveyor of Liverpool admitted that an officer rarely did substitution work for as long as six months.

[3] Evidence, Stanley Committee on Post Office, p. 182.

tribunals, for the Holt Committee recommended that all substitution duty exceeding the ordinary annual leave of the class to which the officer belonged should be paid for at the minimum rate of the class for which he was substituting.[1] In these cases the workers had been made to pay for one of their privileges. In another detail—that of split duties—they suffered in consequence of the nature of their employment and the parsimony of the Department. Owing to the peculiar nature of postal work, it has often been necessary for sorters, postmen, telegraphists, and others to do more than one spell of duty during the day. Instances of as many as five attendances at the office each day have not been infrequent, and these have sometimes covered a total period of fifteen hours.[2] The difficulty is quite an old one, and in 1891 the Department believed that the system was welcome to the men, since it gave them a break in the middle of the day, which was useful either for rest or for earning some addition to their wages.[3] Latterly objection has been taken by the workers, and particularly by postmen, not so much to the fact of split duties as to the extent to which they were carried. Five attendances were regarded as excessive, and it was claimed that the number in the majority of such instances could be reduced if the Department would permit more overtime.[4] That the Department had no intention of increasing its wage-bill for such

[1] Report, Holt Committee on Post Office (H.C. 268 of 1913), par. 70.

[2] Report, Raikes Inquiry, 1891 (unpublished), par. 61. Manchester, Birmingham, Dublin, and Brighton were mentioned as places where the long day existed.

[3] *Ibid.*

[4] Evidence, Hobhouse Committee on Post Office (H.C. 380 of 1907), Qs. 3,510–3.

a purpose is to be seen from the fate of an application submitted by the staff of an Irish office. At Enniskillen application was made for a meal-time relief on a duty on which relief could have been granted. An inquiry was made, and the Department found that by changing the duty from a " two-split " to a " three-split " the meal relief could be avoided. The change was made.[1]

Overtime has always, prior to 1914, been confined within the smallest limits. Not only was it avoided as much as possible by the devices of auxiliary labour and split duties, but when inevitable it was paid for at rates which compare unfavourably with outside employment. Work on Sundays and Bank Holidays was paid for at time and a half. All other overtime was paid for at the ordinary rate, unless it fell between 10 p.m. and 6 a.m., for which the rate was time and a seventh. Sorters in the travelling post offices were paid overtime on a five-weeks' basis, and received extra payment on the usual scale, if their hours of duty in five weeks exceeded 240. This was a necessary arrangement in consequence of the system of allowing sorters on this duty one night's rest in five. The Hobhouse Committee thought it desirable to attempt to combine with this a sort of supplementary payment for an individual trip of unusual duration. Already a " trip allowance " of 3s.—partly out-of-pocket expenses and partly payment for exceptional service —had been granted by the Department. The Committee recommended the payment of an additional 1s. if the officer was absent for more than twelve hours, with further additions of 1s. for each 4 hours

[1] Evidence, Hobhouse Committee on Post Office (H.C. 380 of 1907), Q. 3,514.

up to a total of 20.[1]   For workers on ordinary duties overtime was not placed on a satisfactory footing until after 1914.   In that year the Holt Committee recommended that overtime rates be decided by the total number of hours worked in a week, rising from time and a quarter after 48 hours to time and a half after 54 hours, and double time after 60 hours.[2]   These are quite moderate and reasonable proposals, and they alone are sufficient to indicate how unwilling the Department was for many years, to pay a decent rate for the little overtime it needed.

Cheapness again was the avowed reason of the Post Office for employing female labour.   The Second Secretary of the Department admitted, in 1906, that the reason for changing from men to women for certain duties was that the women were found to be able to do work quite as well and were at the same time cheaper.[3] Even in 1914, after earlier improvements in the scales of female officers, the highest pay of a female sorting clerk and telegraphist of five years' service, in the provinces was only 22s. per week.   That, of course, was not the top of her scale, but for a very large proportion of the women officers it was the most they ever received.   Statements as to the number of women officers, who left the service with from six to twelve years to their credit, showed that the percentage was considerable and fairly constant.   In two successive years, 41 and 31 respectively from a total staff of over 1,000 left the London Central Telegraph Office after

[1] Report, Hobhouse Committee on Post Office (H.C. 266 of 1907), par. 138.
[2] Report, Holt Committee on Post Office (H.C. 268 of 1913), par. 135.
[3] Evidence, Hobhouse Committee on Post Office (H C. 380 of 1907), Qs. 15,733-5.

8

such short service.[1] To women workers as a class the maxima of their scales were of but slight importance. The Department secured the double economy of paying less for female than for male labour, and of rarely having to pay the higher wages which long service would have entailed.

The poorest wages of all have been those of rural postmen. Their work was certainly difficult to organize profitably. Many of them worked in thinly populated areas, and had to walk long distances to carry out comparatively little postal business. Their work illustrates the statement that the postal undertaking is primarily a public service, and only secondarily a profit-making concern. Usually a rural postman started out from a small town and delivered letters on a country " walk " which sometimes extended to twelve miles. On arrival at the terminal point, he waited until the afternoon when he returned to the office from which he started with the collections from offices *en route*.[2] The working day, including the halt after the outward journey, covered the period of from 5 a.m. or 6 a.m. to 7 p.m. or 7.30 p.m., and the wages, even as late as 1903, varied from 12s. to 20s. in England. Some rural postmen in Ireland received only 10s. a week for full-time work. There was practically no change in these wages between 1891 and 1903, and the table on page 115, prepared for the Raikes inquiry in 1891, gives some indication of the allocation of wages during that period.[3]

---

[1] Evidence, Hobhouse Committee on Post Office (H.C. 380 of 1907), Q. 3,320.

[2] Examples of rural " walks " are given in Appendix B.

[3] Report, Raikes Inquiry, 1891 (unpublished), par. 40.

Number of Rural Postmen.

		England and Wales	Scotland	Ireland	Total
	s. d.				
At wages of	10 0	—	—	4	4
,,	11 0	—	—	43	43
,,	12 0	59	3	109	171
,,	13 0	57	7	107	171
,,	14 0	378	29	145	552
,,	15 0	980	88	105	1,173
,,	16 0	1,495	224	70	1,789
,,	17 0	653	119	2	774
,,	18 0	378	74	—	452
,,	19 0	38	1	—	39
,,	20 0	14	2	—	16
		4,052	547	585	5,184

All of these were full-time men. Many of them started on their walks from town offices at which the postmen were paid on higher scales. By 1907 the minimum was 15s. in Ireland and 16s. in the United Kingdom, and the Department urged that this was proper remuneration, on the ground that a postman who had to wait four or five hours at the extreme point of his journey should be able to find some light work to do during the waiting period.[1] These wages were evidently fixed with close reference to the wages of agricultural labourers in the various districts. The postmaster of Belfast in 1906 asserted that the rates were based on the wages of agricultural labourers,[2] and although the Secretary of the Post Office denied this, he admitted that farm wages figures had been collected for the purposes of comparison.[3] Mere comparison indeed was quite unfair, since it could take no

[1] Evidence, Stanley Committee on Post Office (Cd. 2171 of 1904), p. 155.
[2] Evidence, Hobhouse Committee on Post Office (H.C. 380 of 1907), Qs. 9,730-3.
[3] *Ibid.*, Q. 9,917.

account of the value of perquisites, which have frequently been mentioned as an important item in the wages of farm labour.

Naturally the work was not sought after by persons already in the service, and the Post Office found itself faced with two difficulties. If it made the position of rural postmen more attractive by constituting it a medium of promotion it would have fewer vacancies at town post offices for ex-telegraph messengers. Yet, at existing rates, it would not have been easy, before 1907, to persuade telegraph messengers to leave town homes and become rural postmen. No hard-and-fast policy was decided upon, but the postmasters of some towns made it a rule that vacancies on the town staff should be filled from rural postmen working in the surrounding districts.[1] Prospects of this sort did not alter the fact that the wages were low—low often in comparison with the Department's own scales. In 1903 the minimum for a town postman at Birkenhead was 18s., but a country postman working from the same centre would receive only 16s.[2] In comparison with other public servants the discrepancy was greater still. The Postmaster-General in 1904 admitted that there were rural postmen in Devon who had served terms in the army and were paid 16s., though third-class policemen in the same district had wages of 21s.[3]

These, then, are some of the developments of the Department's independence in the labour market. Whether the question be one of scheduling offices without due regard to the effect on real wages, or of fixing rural wages by the standards of an alien industry,

[1] Evidence, Stanley Committee on Post Office (Cd. 2171 of 1904), p. 152.
[2] *Ibid.*
[3] " Hansard," February 9, 1904.

its treatment in the ways described has been possible largely owing to the absence of a competitor or exemplar, who should urge the Department to a thorough examination of its systems. Incidentally, too, the Post Office has reaped some of the benefit of increasing education. Counter work in London was, up to 1879, done by Civil Service clerks, who were paid on a scale rising to £240.[1] In 1903 the same work, with the numerous accretions of a quarter of a century's development, was done by counter clerks with a maximum salary of £160.

If such were the disadvantages of employment in a Government monopoly, it may be said that for half of the employees there were the special advantages of establishment, and for a particular class—postmen—there were additional payments and the provision of uniform. Sick pay, holidays, medical attendance and a pension undoubtedly have a value, and one which varies in proportion to the salary of the worker concerned. A Departmental estimate of the money worth of privileges for a London sorter in 1906 was £21 16s. 7d. per annum.[2] That represents a notable addition to a worker's income, and may truly be said to remove the need for some items of insurance. Unfortunately the acceptance of privileges in lieu of wages is not optional, and, in the case of sorters at all events, the deduction is far heavier than the contributions demanded by the National Health Insurance Act, or by the average trade union, or by both together. The heavy item is that in respect of superannuation, and it is sometimes contended by the workers that

[1] Evidence, Stanley Committee on Post Office (Cd. 2171 of 1904), Q. 598.

[2] Evidence, Hobhouse Committee (H.C. 380 of 1907), Q. 224.

they should not bear the whole cost of this, because it is advantageous to the Department to have a stable staff.[1] The Stanley Committee went much further than this in 1903, and suggested that pension prospects might be set off against the curtailing of the civil rights of Post Office employees.[2] For the postmen an additional consideration is the supply of uniform, and until recently postmen were eligible for good conduct stripes. In 1891 a maximum of three stripes, each worth 1s. per week, and each obtainable after five years' service, was allowed, but they were not unlimited. For every 100 men, 50 badges were allowed —30 three-stripe, 10 two-stripe, and 10 one-stripe [3]— so that a postman's extra pay might depend not only upon his own good service, but upon the behaviour and longevity of his colleagues. By 1897 the limitation had gone, and the good conduct stripes which any one postman might collect had been increased to six. After 1914 they vanished entirely and were merged in wages proper.

All these points serve to amplify the earlier statement that very little attempt has been made by the Post Office to set values upon work. Incremental scales certainly render that difficult, for it is impossible to claim that increments, after the first few years, bear

[1] The Report of the Royal Commission on Superannuation in the Civil Service, par. 10, contains the following : " It is advantageous to the State that part of the remuneration of its servants should take this form, as there is thus secured an inducement to maintain continuous service on the part of the servant and a facility on the part of the State to dispense with further services if age or infirmity renders them less efficient."

[2] Report, Stanley Committee on Post Office (Cd. 2170 of 1904) : General principles.

[3] Raikes Inquiry, 1891 (unpublished), Appendix VI.

any real relationship to the increase in the value of the work done by a particular officer. This was realized by the Committee of 1891. When reminded that in private enterprise most workers, of similar economic grade to that of postman, reached their full wage at the age of 21, the Committee had to conclude that wages in Post Office service must be viewed throughout their whole period—a course which was possible owing to the greater security of Government employment.[1] Following this view, continuity of employment is a moral right, necessary in order to avoid underpayment for work done in earlier years. But it is not only in the matter of scales that incongruous effects are produced. The Comptroller and Accountant-General of the Post Office admitted in 1907 that there were some assistant supervisors in his Department who were receiving from 1s. to 7s. a week less than some of the sorter-tracers whom they supervised.[2] Also when the insufficiency of the starting salaries generally was first attacked in 1903, the concessions made were not based at all upon the value of work but upon the age of the officer. Special increases for all grades were sanctioned for every officer at the age of 25.[3] Within the very wide limits of the schedules based on volume of work the officer was rated and not his work.

The attitude of the workers on these matters has not been to question seriously the ratios maintained between the various grades, or to attack directly the supply and demand basis. Only indirectly have they approached this question by criticizing the low minima

[1] Report, Raikes Inquiry, 1891 (unpublished), par. 19.
[2] Evidence, Hobhouse Committee on Post Office (H.C. 380 of 1907), Qs. 2,564–5.
[3] Memorandum by Postmaster-General on the Report of the Stanley Committee, issued March 24, 1905.

and long scales, and by taunting the Department with the charge of paying " pocket-money " wages to women.[1] They have been compelled by the attitude of the Department to seek comparisons outside the service. None of these has been very satisfactory or very effective, and the workers have concentrated on demands that real wages be maintained, that minima shall be at least high enough to maintain an adult, that rates shall not be cut by economy devices, and that overtime shall be paid for at appropriate rates.

A programme of this sort would appear to involve necessarily a large measure of collective bargaining. And negotiations with the workers as a body was anathema to the Department. Organization of Post Office grades was of comparatively early date. The homogeneity of each class favoured it, but the obtaining of recognition of the men's unions by the Department was a far less easy matter. For complete recognition postal servants have to thank the abnormal conditions brought about by the war. In the early years of this century the unions were strong and extraordinarily active, and since the path of collective bargaining was closed to them they turned their attention to the work of compelling the Department to move, through its masters—the Commons.

Probably no agitation for Parliamentary action has been so vigorously, almost ruthlessly pressed. The organization of postal workers was so efficient that few Members of Parliament escaped badgering. Many were readily sympathetic, and these were generously primed with facts and figures for use in the House. Those who turned a deaf ear were made the objects of

[1] Evidence, Hobhouse Committee (H.C. 380 of 1907), Q. 3,304.

steady and continuous pressure, varying from appeals
for fair treatment to threats as to their fate at the
next election. As early as April, 1903, Mr. Austen
Chamberlain, then Postmaster-General, spoke publicly
of the unwelcome activities of postal servants, and
confessed that Members of Parliament had applied to
him for protection. Here is his statement : " I have
had members come to me, not from one side of the
House alone, to seek from me, in my position as
Postmaster-General, protection for them in the
discharge of their public duties against the pressure
sought to be put upon them by employees of the Post
Office." [1] In the following year the attack had
advanced to another stage, and deputations of as many
as forty Members of Parliament were being organized
to approach the Postmaster-General in the interests
of postal workers. [2] In 1903 the main desire of the
agitators was that a Select Committee should be set
up. So confident were the workers that they
announced their willingness to accept the decisions of
such a Committee. [3] So impressed was the Postmaster-
General with the coercion of members that he dared
not appoint a Select Committee of members. Mr.
Chamberlain agreed to an inquiry of " very limited
scope " by a Committee appointed from outside the
House. [4] That Committee sat and its recommendations came before Lord Stanley, the successor
of Mr. Chamberlain, at the head of the Post Office.
The recommendations involved an additional
expenditure of a million pounds a year, [5] and

[1] " Hansard," April 30, 1903.
[2] Ibid., August 9, 1904 : Speech of Mr. Henniker Heaton.
[3] Ibid., April 30, 1903 : Speech of Mr. T. Bayley.
[4] Ibid., April 30, 1903.
[5] Ibid., August 9, 1904 : Speech of Lord Stanley.

Lord Stanley first temporized, and then defiantly announced that he would not accept the Committee's report but would bring forward a scheme which he thought desirable.[1]   The torrent, which had been only partially released during the period of delay between the issuing of the Committee's report and the declaration of the Postmaster-General, again deluged the the official head.   Questions as to Post Office matters were raised at every sitting, and postal workers resumed their practice of issuing political threats.   Lord Stanley, quoting one of these circulars [2] in the House, described it as "nothing more or less than blackmail." [3] This raised a fresh storm of protest—a telegram to the Postmaster-General from the telegraphists, and a general assault in the House.   Lord Stanley stood firm, and the general election of December, 1905, saved him from a very awkward situation, and handed on the problem to a new Ministry, which immediately appointed a Select Committee of Members of Parliament—the Hobhouse Committee—to inquire into all postal wages.

Were there not so serious a side to activity of this sort, the situation would be quite Gilbertian.   A body of men who were restrained by numerous regulations from active participation in politics, who could not be candidates for election to the House of Commons, or make speeches at election meetings, or even serve

---

[1] "Hansard," March 13 1905.
[2] The objectionable paragraph: "Two-thirds at least of one political party are in great fear of losing their seats.   The swing of the pendulum is against them and any member who receives forty or fifty such letters will, under present circumstances, have to consider very seriously whether on this question he can afford to go into the wrong lobby.   This is taking advantage of the political situation."
[3] "Hansard," July 6, 1905.

on election committees, who could not, at that time, contest municipal elections, had used the Parliamentary machine to embarrass the Postmaster-General and to " intimidate " members of the House.[1] The precedent created was a bad one. It seemed as though democratic government could be manipulated in the interests of a small section of the community, and at the expense of the nation as a whole. The particular case, however, was justifiable on the ground that the workers had real grievances and could find no way of getting them dealt with except through the House of Commons. Years before, when a section of the postal employees had sought to use the workers' only effective weapon—the strike—it had not only failed, but had also evoked from the Treasury a threat of legislation to cover the Post Office, similar to that which protects public services such as gas and water supplies from interruption by " breaches of contracts of service." [2] "If the existing Post Office Acts do not meet this case," wrote the Treasury to the Postmaster-General, in 1881, " it will be for My Lords to consider whether the circumstances continue to be such as to make it their duty to propose to Parliament an extension to the Post Office of provisions similar to those cited above. . . ." [3]

The inability of the workers to move otherwise, since the Department refused to negotiate with trade union representatives,[4] practically excuses the application of Parliamentary pressure. Yet it involved a

[1] " Hansard," August 9, 1904 (Mr. Henniker Heaton), and July 6, 1905 (Mr. Ritchie).

[2] 38 and 39 Vic., cap. 86, sec. 4.

[3] Letter included in Report of the Fawcett Inquiry on Post Office, 1881 (unpublished).

[4] " Hansard," July 18, 1905 : Answer of Lord Stanley to Mr. Keir Hardie.

danger, which has not recurred, because no Postmaster-General since then has flouted the recommendations of a Select Committee, and there seemed to have developed before the war a tacit agreement between workers and Department that reference to a Select Committee should be in effect reference to arbitration. The workers would contend that the recommendations of committees have been evaded by less obvious methods,[1] but at all events they can justly claim that only under pressure have improvements been conceded. Out of the struggle, which went on from 1903 to 1914, some good things emerged. Regard to the cost of living has modified the " unit " system schedules since 1907,[2] and the idea of allowing the workers decent pay at the " age of responsibility " has followed that. In the first excitement at the wrangling over the Stanley Report the Department seems to have been unduly impressed by the workers' demands for promotion prospects. It is evident that unnecessary overseerships were made for a certain number of sorting clerks and telegraphists.[3] This the Department denied, probably in order to avoid its being taken as a precedent, but it is certainly true that counter clerks with the status of overseers were subsequently doing ordinary counter work alongside men of the lower grade.[4]   The pressure has also brought a fairly large degree of standardization in the matter of wages. Rural postmen since 1907 have received the same wages as the postmen working in the towns from

[1] *Supra*, p. 108.
[2] Report, Hobhouse Committee on Post Office (H.C. 266 of 1907), par. 256.
[3] Evidence, Hobhouse Committee on Post Office (H.C. 380 of 1907), Q. 5,873 and p. 452. See also Report, Hobhouse Committee (H.C. 266 of 1907), par. 219.
[4] Evidence, Hobhouse Committee on Post Office, p. 439.

which the rural postmen set out. Individual grievances of long duration have similarly yielded. An
overworked superintendent at the South-West London
District Office was given relief (after more than two
years' delay) on the day before his case was laid before
the Holt Committee.[1]

Changes in the Post Office have always been made
especially difficult by the need to respect the vested
interests of existing classes. The Hobhouse Committee
evidently felt that it could have made many improvements if it had not been impeded by this tradition.[2]
Those interests have been very largely respected by
the Department. They are a part of its system, yet
the recommendation of the Holt Committee, that they
should be confined to insuring to each individual that
the rate of pay, hours of work, and privileges should
be equivalent to what was officially held out to him[3]
was a wise limitation. The question has stood in the
way of standardization and of advantageous reorganization.

In recent years the attitude of the Department to
wages generally has not changed much. The Holt
Committee was directed in 1913 to have " regard, . . .
as far as may be, to the standard rate of wages and the
positions of other classes of workers."[4] The Depart-

[1] Report, Holt Committee on Post Office (H.C. 268 of 1913),
par. 131.

[2] Report, Hobhouse Committee on Post Office (H.C. 266
of 1907). Par. 115 says : " Your Committee would have
desired to be free to suggest a complete and total revision of
the compartments into which the postal service is divided. . . .
But with time the vested interests of existing classes have grown
to such an extent that it would be unfair to large numbers
of the staff to disturb them without grave reason."

[3] Report, Holt Committee on Post Office (H.C. 268 of 1913),
pars. 12, 13.

[4] *Ibid.* par. 14.

ment was still looking for an outside comparison, which it must have known could not be found. The wage-rates fixed by the Committee were founded on a more definite basis. Their report declares that consideration had been given to the value of the work to be done, the cost of living, and a reasonable standard of comfort.[1] The outbreak of war prevented the rapid application of the Committee's recommendations, but these have formed the subject of negotiations since the war.

As to the remarkable attraction exercised by the Service there can be no doubt. Only occasionally has the supply of labour fallen short in any department, and then usually because of serious industrial upheaval such as is caused by a war. From 1900 to 1904 there were 3,087 candidates for appointment to the position of postmen for whom there were only 695 vacancies.[2] For the higher grades a steady flow of candidates is maintained from special educational establishments and from the secondary schools of all large towns. Here, as in the case of Civil Service candidates, there is a certain wastage, which increases in volume as competition for appointment becomes keener. Theoretically the Department still decides its wages according to supply and demand,[3] but this is tempered now by the fact that tardy recognition of the postal

[1] Report, Holt Committee on Post Office (H.C. 268 of 1913), pars. 15–17.

[2] "Hansard," July 6, 1905 (Lord Stanley).

[3] Report, Holt Committee on Post Office (H.C. 268 of 1913), par. 14 : "Moreover, the evidence shows clearly that with the exception of a few of the more highly skilled branches of the engineering department during periods of abnormal expansion of work, there is no difficulty in recruiting a sufficient number of persons competent for the duties they have to perform."

trade unions has made collective bargaining possible. Even to-day no outside union is " recognized," and it is sheer good fortune for the Post Office that its workers were never attracted to any appreciable extent to general labour unions. Otherwise the Post Office would have had to face the same problem as that which the Admiralty met, and would probably have failed, as did the Admiralty, to isolate its labour from that of the outside world. Postal workers are very well organized in their own unions, and with the help of the Whitley Councils are at least protected from most of the disadvantages from which they suffered in the past.

It may be concluded that, for the greater part of their history, Post Office wages have been based on supply and demand. They were fixed by the Department at levels which would secure the type of labour required for the various classes of work. Beyond this the Department has used its monopolist position to depress wages in the course of their application to particular conditions. The payment for most overtime at a flat rate, the failure to remunerate officers for long spells of substitution duty, the excessive use of cheap auxiliary and assistant labour, the payment of low wages to rural postmen, and the retention of unappointed learners for long periods are all instances of this abuse. The workers strove to meet this with a countervailing monopoly of labour in the form of trade unions, and for a time failed owing to the refusal of the Department to treat with them. They were forced to use the political weapon, and they met with such unusual success that redress of grievances, and ultimately the right of collective bargaining, emerged.

The attempt of the Department to apply the

principle of payment by results under its scheme of " unit of work " schedules is not very convincing. Its effects are really so slightly related to work values that the description " payment by results " is not justified, and the claim of the Department in 1907 that it resulted in the maintenance of real wages suggested that excuses for the system were difficult to find, and also involved, for the first time, an implicit admission of the importance of the cost of living. It is evidently not easy to apply piecework systems in Government employment of this kind, though if comparison with private industry is made it is not obvious that a piece-list for the major operations of Post Office work presents any more obstacles than piece-lists for the textile or boot manufacturing industries.

The practice of paying for status rather than for actual work is most strongly marked in the Post Office, and the existence of this tendency throughout Government employment suggests a certain inevitableness. Under the present system a degree of continuity is morally assured, and definite terms are fixed on appointment. The element of " contract " in this undoubtedly renders it difficult, after appointment, to make earnings correspond to output.   There are indications of movements in this direction, but they are partial and inconclusive, and aim merely at stopping progression if an officer is inefficient.   There have been "efficiency bars" in incremental scales for many years. They have most often not meant much, but the present tendency to develop the spirit which those regulations embodied may have interesting results.

CHAPTER V

RECENT DEVELOPMENTS

THE war, with the vast expansion of Government employment and the need of the State to deal with huge numbers of well-organized workers, made negotiations or their substitute—arbitration—inevitable. The Committee on Production drifted quickly into the position of an arbitrator in the affairs of industrial establishments. In May, 1917, the Civil Service Arbitration Board was set up to deal with the claims of non-manual workers in Government employment. Before such tribunals, departmental representatives and trade union officials gave evidence on equal terms. Awards were made ; in many cases agreements between Department and workers were registered by these courts of arbitration. The old state of affairs had passed. Under the pressure of need, the Government at one step separated its functions as sovereign from those of its Departments as employers. Except that it had the advantage of protective legislation, the Government submitted, as an ordinary employer, to all the incidents of the collective bargain. Even before the war the barriers had begun to give way. Deputations to Cabinet Ministers or departmental chiefs had been merged in something approaching negotiation. The Admiralty " received " workpeople's representatives at Whitehall and paid their expenses. Trade union officials approached

9 129

directly the Superintendents of War Office Factories. The Office of Works had agreed to accept the terms which collective bargaining " outside " produced. War emergencies provided the pressure necessary to make tendencies into acknowledged policy. Hence negotiations during the war were definitely arranged, and the resort to force on either side was avoided by three devices—arbitration, restrictive legislation, and the promise of a Restoration of Pre-War Practices Act when the emergency should have passed.

Arbitration was clearly a necessity if production were to be carried on without interruption, but in all questions of remuneration it was the aim of the Government during the war period, to confine negotiations to the maintenance of real wages. By legislative restrictions the ordinary influences of supply and demand were prevented from operating, and, in simple justice, it was necessary to provide machinery for adjusting wages to the cost of living. After the passing of the Munitions Act of 1915 the Committee on Production became the tribunal which was to perform this service. Circumstances were to prove too strong, subsequently, for the Government to adhere rigidly to its original intention. New types of labour appeared and new bases had to be found for the wages of such types. The arbitration bodies, which were set up before the end of the war, indicate broadly the special problems which intruded. The Special Arbitration Tribunal for Women, and the Special Arbitration Tribunal on Unskilled Men's Wages represent two of the difficulties on the manual labour side ; and the Civil Service Arbitration and Conciliation Board, set up in February, 1917, is the belated attempt to deal with Government Departments separately and apart from the mass of labour engaged on munitions work.

For both types of labour the Government was responsible during this period, and its wage-standards are worthy of attention. The cost of living basis adopted by the Committee on Production, for manual workers, sufficed only until the shrinkage of the normal labour supply brought the need for labour of new types. Skilled men became fewer in numbers and in proportion to the skilled work which had to be done. The shortage had to be met by the adaptation of machines for operation by semi-skilled men and by women. Most of this work had never been allotted wages in peace time, and the arbitration tribunal had to find a means of fixing remuneration for these new classes. The result was to produce still further proof of the value of collective bargaining, particularly in the matter of women's wages. In the case of semi-skilled men the possibility of high earnings under piecework systems masked to a very great extent the disparity between the rates they received and those which would have been paid, under pre-war systems of factory organization, for similar work. The rates for such work were rarely " agreed." There was a considerable element of arbitrariness in the methods of fixing. The conditions of mass production, under which semi-skilled workers operated machines which were " tooled " by fully skilled men, raised fresh questions as to the maintaining of a reasonable ratio between the earnings of different grades of labour. Very largely these difficulties were of but temporary importance, for the prophesied tendency to mass production in this country does not seem to have materialized since the war.[1]

The question of women's wages during the war has

[1] See G. D. H. Cole's " Trade Unionism and Munitions," Chap. XIV.

a general interest. Deductions from wage-rates on account of additional supervision and the cost of tool setting could not wholly explain the difference between the wages of men and women who did similar work. " Women were, as a rule," writes Mr. G. D. H. Cole, " paid considerably less than men during the war, even on identical jobs, and were often paid less for identical amounts of work on systems of ' payment by results.' " [1] The undefined distinction between the wages of men and of women remained, therefore, and not even the famous " Treasury Agreement," [2] which promised on behalf of the Government that the admission of female labour should not " affect adversely the rates customarily paid for the job," prevented women in the engineering trade from being paid wages equal to about half those of men. [3] In fact, it was not until the autumn of 1915 that a minimum of £1 per week was fixed for women in engineering shops. [4] The progress of women's wages throughout was slow, and the higher standards were only reached ' by persistent trade union effort and in the face of a chorus of complaints that the women were being paid ' more than they were worth.' " [5] Despite restrictions on labour activity trade union effort counted for much. Not only did it bring improvements in the rates for female labour, but it also successfully resisted the attempt of the Government to introduce payment by results in all trades for the duration of the war. [6] The main

[1] See G. D. H. Cole's " Trade Unionism and Munitions," Chap. XIV.
[2] March, 1915.
[3] Barbara Drake : " Women in the Engineering Trade."
[4] *Ibid.*
[5] Cole : " Trade Unionism and Munitions," Chap. XIV.
[6] *Ibid.*, Chap. IX : " This attempt broke down in face of the opposition of the majority of unions of skilled workers."

object of this design was, undoubtedly, to stimulate production, but it contained no provision against the danger that high *earnings* under piecework systems might cover inadequate *rates*, i.e. rates less than those the workers were justified, by dilution promises, in expecting.

Of more direct importance, for the purposes of this study, is the treatment of the regular Government employees during this time. For manual labour, wages were varied, chiefly in accordance with changes in the cost of living, by the Committee on Production. For non-manual labour and those classes of labour which were peculiar to Government employment, the Civil Service Arbitration Board began to issue awards in May, 1917. This body found it necessary to decide matters which the general tribunals hardly touched at all. It had to consider how far up in the scale wages should be maintained at their absolute ratio with those of lower grades. It sought to discover how far the wages of highly paid officers were really reduced by a rise in the cost of living. Through a series of variations the Board arrived at a gradation, which the workers themselves accepted, in the spirit of compromise, despite its wide distinctions. The final award, issued in October, 1919, gave graded bonuses ranging from 140 per cent. on pre-war salaries up to £91 5s. a year; to 42 per cent. on those from £200 to £500 a year.[1] The Arbitration Board partially justified these distinctions, by describing the higher officials as sharing " in the national burden by foregoing full compensation for the decrease in the purchasing power of money." That clearly means that the question had not been scientifically explored

[1] Awards and Agreements, Civil Service Arbitration Board, Award 101.

by the Board. The workers themselves went very carefully into the matter and laid much data before the arbitrators. Finally they accepted the arrangement as a compromise, and in the same spirit accepted a very similar basis when their new Whitley Council machinery began to deal with the problem. They, too, laid stress on the sacrificial aspect, and pointed to the extra burden laid on the highly paid man by the increased income tax.[1] Nevertheless, with the cost of living index at 130 above the pre-war level, they agreed to the following scale of bonuses : [2]

For the first	£91 5s.	-	130 per cent.
Next sum up to £200		-	60 ,,
Next sum up to £500		-	45 ,,

Already the Arbitration Board had dealt, still more stringently, with officers receiving from £500 to £1,500, by awarding them bonuses of 10 per cent. plus £25 a year, with the intimation that these gratuities were "intended *to assist* in meeting the increased cost of living." [3]

None of these arrangements appears to have arisen from the establishment or acknowledgment of definite economic principles. They are based explicitly or implicitly, upon the view that all citizens should render some special tribute to the commonwealth in time of stress, except those whose possessions barely sufficed for their human needs. But they also seem to mark a vaguely defined point, above which absolute wage ratios may not be maintained. This

[1] Report of Committee on Cost of Living, appointed by the National Whitley Council of the Civil Service (1920), par. 3.

[2] *Ibid.*

[3] Awards and Agreements, Civil Service Arbitration Board, Vol. I, p. 79.

depends partly upon a restricted view of the word
" living " and its significance, and upon a failure to
include within its definition all the activities of the
worker. It points also to the absence of a definite
recognition of the various standards of living which
different wages have involved, and separates the value
of certain higher classes of labour from the types of
material comfort to which the vendor of that labour has
become accustomed.

This brief examination gives the key to the treatment
of Government employees' wages generally during
the war. The lowest-paid servants had their rates
increased eventually, in proportion to the rise in the
cost of living. The variations did not, until the later
stages, follow closely upon changes in the Ministry of
Labour's index figure. Many classes, who were slow
in bringing their cases to arbitration, found themselves
left far behind in the matter of real wages,[1] but when
wage claims were made, the general basis from which
the tribunal started was the cost of living. Here and
there exceptions to this rule occurred. In June, 1919,
customs and excise surveyors were granted an increase
of £25 a year, in recognition of " additional responsibilities," [2] and an agreement between the Treasury
and the associations of temporary clerks and typists,
approved by the Board in May, 1919, admitted the
principle of " age pay." [3]   Some Post Office rearrangements were also made, with the sanction of the Board,
under the recommendations of the Holt Committee.[4]
Reformation on a large scale was left until after the

[1] Awards and Agreements, Civil Service Arbitration Board,
Vol. I, p. 93. Until April, 1919, temporary clerks of the
Ministry of Labour in Ireland, receiving basic wages of 35s.
a week, had bonuses of only 14s. a week.
[2] Ibid., p. 170. [3] Ibid., p. 105. [4] Ibid., A 6, A 7, A 8.

war, and even the claim of temporary postmen and postwomen, in March, 1918, that they should be paid the average weekly wage of the permanent postmen, was rejected by the Arbitration Board.[1]

Women were almost invariably awarded smaller bonuses, *pro rata*, than men. The distinction between women and men was made in one of the earliest awards, when even the lowest grades of women officers received bonuses at least 25 per cent. lower than those given to men,[2] and a distinction which varied with different classes was maintained throughout. For women, whose salaries were from £500 to £1,500, the final bonus award was " a sum equivalent to two-thirds of the amount payable to men receiving an equal salary." [3] Salaries, therefore, suffered in two respects when their recipients happened to be women. They were not increased to the full extent of the rise in the cost of living, nor were they increased in equal proportion to those of men. No justification for such a policy in regard to low-salaried officers can readily be found. As to the better paid workers, it was apparently the view of the Board that such high wages for women were already so far in excess of the needs of the workers and of the standard required for full efficiency that they were outside the range of mechanical adjustment in response to changing money values.

Only to a very slight extent, then, were the wage-bases of permanent employees altered. The wages themselves were adjusted ; the rates remained almost unchanged, but the new element of free negotiation and arbitration between the workers and the State as an employer meant a change of outlook. The way to

---

[1] Awards and Agreements, Civil Service Arbitration Board, Vol. I, p. 42.   [2] *Ibid.*, p. 9.   [3] *Ibid.*, p. 79.

open collective bargaining was conveniently cleared. The State, without loss of dignity or authority, had " dealt " with labour. It had now to face the difficulties of reconstruction and prepare against the dangers, which the restoration to labour of its weapons might precipitate. Machinery for industrial conciliation seemed a necessity if peace-time production were to be resumed by the country as a whole. Friction, it was felt, would thus be minimized and the readjustment of industry facilitated. With the object of placing such machinery at the disposal of all workers and employers the Whitley Committee was appointed before the end of the war. The Joint Industrial Councils, which the Committee proposed, are now a familiar adjunct of industrial organization. In offering the device to the nation, the Government, as the biggest employer of the moment, could hardly evade the obligation of setting an example by adopting Whitley Councils for its own establishments. But also, the employing Departments *needed* conciliation machinery. The volume and nature of the arbitration business in relation to Government Departments gave an indication of the labour activity which might be expected when pre-war practices were restored. The State as an employer had, for five years, been treating with its industrial workers in the ordinary fashion of an employer. There could obviously be no immediate resumption of the old attitude. This was so evident that the Government may be acquitted of the charge of adopting Whitley Councils for its industrial establishments, mainly with a view to popularizing them. To this desire may only be attributed the fact that they adopted them so early.

The Whitley Committee completed its work in

October, 1917.[1] On July 1st, 1918, the War Cabinet decided " to adopt in principle the application of the recommendations of the Whitley Report, with any necessary adaptations to Government Industrial Establishments, where the conditions were sufficiently analogous to those existing in outside industries." [2] It was not the intention, however, to take the untried system without special safeguards. Admittedly, State employment is different from that of private enterprise —different chiefly in the type of ultimate authority for giving or withholding employment. Hence the War Cabinet further resolved " to set up an Inter-Departmental Committee to consider what modifications [of the Whitley scheme] were necessary." [3] This was a very apprehensive Committee, anxious lest ministerial responsibility should be threatened, and impressed with the need for protecting Treasury control. There was really but little foundation for these fears. They resolve themselves, upon examination, into questions of co-ordination. Ministerial responsibility could only be destroyed if departmental representatives on a Whitley Council acted without the authority of the Minister they represented. The Treasury would not be ignored, so long as it consented to send a member to the Council. The addition of an official from the Ministry of Labour would ensure uniformity and adherence to the line of labour policy agreed upon by the Government. By so arranging the constitutions of the Whitley Councils most of these difficulties were met. In arranging the new machinery a departure was made from the Committee's recommendations.

[1] Supplementary Report of Committee on Relations between Employers and Employed, Cd. 9001 (1918).
[2] Joint Industrial Councils Bulletin, No. 3, September, 1920.
[3] Ibid.

No National Council was set up, nor was one set of organizations allowed to deal with all the questions which labour involves.   It was decided that Departmental Councils should be formed (with the usual subsidiary formations) to deal with " conditions " only. Wages, having regard to the strong craft distinctions which industry has developed, were to be the special care of " Trade Councils," embracing not simply a Government Department but all Departments employing workers of the particular trade.   For this purpose the manual workers were divided into four main groups —engineering, shipbuilding, building, and general labour—and four Trade Councils regulate the wages of all such workers in Government employment.   The craft divisions are, of course, emphasized by this arrangement, and the danger of united action, by all the industrialists at any Government establishment, is made more remote.   Yet there is good foundation for such a remark as the following by Sir Robert Horne : " I know . . . if it came to a question of boilermakers' wages in a Government shipyard, the boilermakers would not thank shipwrights or blacksmiths for any advice they might give." [1] The effect of the scheme is not really to divide the bargain into two sections.   Some of the representatives who attend the Departmental Councils meet again at the Trade Councils.   The transactions of both types of Council are part of the whole process.   Whether equal results could not have been attained without the construction of such ponderous machinery may justly be questioned, and is indeed doubted by some of the officials who help to work the scheme.

[1] Speech at Conference on the Application of the Whitley Report to Government Industrial Establishments, February 20, 1919 (Ministry of Labour Report).

Probably the best stimulus to the new system was to be found in the changed relationship of the Treasury to the various employing Departments. Previously the Treasury had stood apart, setting certain limits to particular items of expenditure, occasionally vetoing proposed increases, and never coming into close touch with the conditions out of which the need for higher costs arose. The absence of close contact must have been felt by the Treasury almost as keenly as by the spending Departments At all events, the Treasury officials took up the scheme whole-heartedly. The conservative aloofness was now to go. Treasury officials were to come down into the thick of the negotiations. The veto was to be removed ! So, at least, Sir Malcolm Ramsay told a conference which considered the scheme. " Some speakers seem to be under the impression that the Treasury veto will go on just as before, and you rightly ask what is the good of having Whitley Councils if this state of things is to continue. Speaking deliberately for the Treasury, I may say our only wish is to carry out the wishes of the Government, that is, to have co-operation and avoid disputes." [1] The Treasury officials were to attend Council meetings with powers to act, within certain limits, and, in the event of disagreement, the Treasury were " perfectly agreeable to go to arbitration." [2]

The process of convincing the Treasury that it must no longer issue decrees from afar had been a difficult one, although in adopting the new attitude it was merely coming into line with ordinary employers. The Inter-Departmental Committee, which evolved

[1] Speech at Conference on the Application of the Whitley Report to Government Industrial Establishments, February 20, 1919 (Ministry of Labour Report).
[2] *Ibid.*

the details of the undertaking, realized this. Here is its view : " So far as it applies to wages negotiations, the Whitley Report appears to endorse what has for years been the recognized practice of well-regulated trades, viz. the arrangement of terms between bodies representative of, and able to make final settlements for, the employers and employed respectively." And its appreciation of the need for modernizing Treasury control is seen in the following : " Unless the whole outlook of the Whitley Report is wrong, it is to be presumed that the opportunity of discussion with Treasury officials would produce in the trade unions an understanding and appreciation of the Treasury attitude, which otherwise cannot be expected."[1] Such modernization is simply to make Treasury actions intelligible and less apparently arbitrary. Theoretically, the Treasury thus waives its right to veto, though actually it still holds the power to prevent agreement and so compel resort to arbitration. It is fair to note, however, that any representative on a Whitley Council holds this power, for it is provided generally that decisions must also be agreements, and may not be arrived at by the vote of a majority.[2] The Treasury is in the stronger position of being able to take independent executive action and to block any proposal for amendment which might be raised at a Council meeting. Where disagreement concerned wages it was stipulated that it should be referred to the Industrial Court. Other matters in which agreement is not reached have no definite machinery of arbitration, though informal consultation by the chairman and vice-chairman of a

[1] Official Summary, Report of Inter-Departmental Committee on the Application of the Whitley Report to Government Industrial Establishments, par. 9.

[2] Constitutions of Government Joint Industrial Councils.

Council is urged. This looks like a weak point, yet the Councils so far have worked remarkably well and have got through a large amount of business. The Admiralty Council in 1919 approved a scheme for reducing the dockyards to a peace footing, with as little hardship as possible.[1] The Office of Works, having practically no workshops in the ordinary sense, set to work to organize " shop " committees by trades in certain sections, with similar organizations for the larger divisions under the name of " works " committees.[2] Only the War Office Council seems to have failed to enlist the sympathy of some of its workers. The employees at Woolwich have so far refused to send representatives, and the council operates without them.

Yet it was not, in every case, a foregone conclusion that the trade unions should be the medium of expression for the democratic spirit. The Admiralty has never welcomed trade union intrusion, and though it admitted union representatives to negotiations before the war, it would much have preferred to do without them and to deal direct with its workers. The Board actually sought, just before the end of the war, to set up machinery which would have made negotiations, for every dockyard, separate and distinct, and would have excluded from such negotiations the officials of the unions. This was embodied in a scheme published by the Commissioners on May 13, 1918, proposing to establish shop committees and a yard committee for every dockyard. Up to a point, this was a following out of the recommendations of the Whitley Committee, which had reported finally in October, 1917. It anticipated by six weeks the

[1] Joint Industrial Councils Bulletin, No. 2, December, 1919.
[2] *Ibid.*

formal decision of the Cabinet to apply the Whitley
scheme to Government industrial establishments.

It proposed that one shop committee should be
formed for each trade, and one " for each large trade
which is not included in a shop." The intended
functions of each shop committee were set forth
thus : " It is thought that (a) questions affecting
warming and lighting of shops, and others generally
affecting the well-being and comfort of employees ;
(b) questions relating to output, recording, piecework
prices, etc. ; and (c) questions relating to dilution,
are among those which will probably be discussed by
shop committees." [1] The yard committees were to
deal with all matters submitted to them " by any of
the shop committees or by heads of departments."
The committees were, in fact, to operate in the manner
suggested by the Whitley Committee, but whereas
the latter body made it a condition that such
machinery should rest upon a foundation of thorough
organization, the Admiralty scheme proposed to start
from a basis of absolute democracy and to ignore
the existing organizations of the workers. Representatives on both types of committee were to be
elected by secret ballot of all the workers in a shop
for the shop committee, and of all the workers in the
dockyard for the yard committee. Members of shop
committees were to be eligible for election to the
yard committee, but the only persons who might be
nominated for the shop committee were those who
had served " not less than five years in civilian
employment under the Admiralty." The trade unions

[1] This scheme was published by the Admiralty under the
reference number D. 10,902/1918, and circulated to the
dockyards for consideration and criticism by the workers
(May 18, 1918).

concerned were not only ignored, but were thus cut off from the affairs of each yard. No attempt was made, in this scheme, to erect machinery which would co-ordinate action in all yards, but possible developments were hinted at.

The scheme was never tried out. Keen opposition was offered by the unions, especially by the A.S.E., and eventually the Admiralty gave way in favour of the Government's scheme of Joint Industrial Councils. The attempt is proof of the disfavour with which some of the Departments have looked upon organized labour. Whitleyism arrived nevertheless, and has worked quite as well as might have been hoped.

All these arrangements, it must be noted, applied only to the industrial establishments and the industrial workers of the Government. Administrative, professional, and clerical employees were still left without any conciliation machinery. These classes had been the most reasonable and the least troublesome during the war, and had not even demanded bonuses equal to the full rise in the cost of living until 1919. Consequently they were not catered for in the Government's first scheme. There can be no doubt, too, that the Cabinet would not voluntarily have offered a Whitley Council system. The decision to extend the principle of conciliation to Civil Servants was conceded grudgingly, after insistent demands, and when agitation rendered it impossible longer to ignore the wishes of the non-manual workers in this respect, the measure of Whitleyism offered was pale and unsatisfying.

The sub-committee appointed finally by the Inter-Departmental Committee to draw up a scheme for the Civil Service proper was extremely anxious to set safeguards. It felt that the fact that the State was the ultimate employer limited freedom of action on the part of heads of Departments. It regarded Treasury control as the equivalent of the " check imposed by considerations of profit and loss " in private industry. And it tried hard to reinforce the old contention that a civil servant was first a servant of the public and secondly a wage-earner.[1] Clearly, there is good reason for the existence of a Treasury or some equivalent check, since the automatic penalty which follows uneconomical expenditure in private business cannot follow in Government Departments. Bankruptcy, in the ordinary sense, cannot result from extravagance in administration, and unsound conditions may persist until some public investigation brings amendment. It seemed unlikely, however, that conciliation proceedings could induce the Treasury to forget its responsibility.

The sub-committee was extremely afraid, also, that

[1] Report of Civil Service Sub-Committee of the Inter-Departmental Committee on the Application of the Whitley Report to Government Establishments, par. 7.
" Among the principal differences are :—
" (1) The fact that the State is the ultimate employer of Government servants through the Heads of Departments who consequently have not the freedom of decision in regard to wages and conditions enjoyed by the private employer.
" (2) The absence of check imposed by considerations of profit and loss, and its replacement by Treasury control, which, so far as questions of remuneration are concerned, is now (1918) subject to an appeal to the Conciliation and Arbitration Board for Government employees.
" (3) The fact that an employee in a Government office is not merely a private individual in public employment, but is in a very real sense a servant of the public, and, as such, has assumed obligations which, to some extent, necessarily limit his ordinary rights as a private citizen."

10

the workers might form an exaggerated estimate of the influence they would be able to exert through Joint Industrial Councils.   " It is possible," the sub-committee reported, " that the scheme may have received support under the impression that its adoption will give civil servants a deciding voice in the settlement of their own remuneration and conditions of service." [1]   Any hopes of this kind were finally dealt with by the declaration that the Councils " must be consultative and must not be invested with any executive functions." [2]   This provision condemned the scheme—generally known as the " Heath Report "—and the opposition, organized by the Civil Service Confederation, made it evident that some more effective measure of conciliation must be conceded.   Eventually the work of drawing up a plan for Civil Service Whitley Councils was placed in the hands of a joint committee, composed of representatives from the " official " side and from the Civil Service associations. Thus it was practically a Joint Industrial Council which planned the Council system of the Civil Service. Their proposals included the setting up of a national council, departmental councils, and district or office committees.   The separation of wage questions from other negotiations was not attempted, as in the case of the councils for industrial workers ;   and the original desire that such bodies should be merely consultative, was duly buried beneath the following paragraph :   " The decisions of the Council shall be arrived at by agreement between the two sides . . . shall be reported to the Cabinet, and thereupon shall

[1] Report of Civil Service Sub-Committee of the Inter-Departmental Committee on the Application of the Whitley Report to Government Establishments, par. 5.
[2] *Ibid.*, par. 46 (b).

become operative." [1] This report provided for full collective bargaining, with the reference of disputed wages questions to the Civil Service Arbitration Board, and was approved by the War Cabinet in June, 1919 [2]—just a year after the resolution to apply Whitleyism to Government industrial establishments.

Many of the apprehensions which the " official " side experienced with regard to the new system, have vanished. One of the gravest fears entertained was readily set at rest by the National Council. Since the ready-made scheme had been rejected and the Joint Council had imposed one of its own preparation, it seemed necessary to restate the position of the existing authorities. The " official " side was anxious to have an affirmation that the power of heads of Departments was not regarded as having been put in commission, and that the final authority rested with Parliament. The " staff " side offered no objection to this definition, nor has any action of the Council since then impeded the freedom of departmental chiefs in arriving at decisions and acting upon them.

Since its establishment this organization has dealt energetically with a number of problems. The National Whitley Council of the Civil Service had greater opportunities for reorganization than any other conciliation body concerned with Government employment. It has also the longest list of achievements. By the aid of sub-committees it produced a

[1] Report of the National Provisional Joint Committee on the Application of the Whitley Report to the Administrative Departments of the Civil Service (Cmd. 198 of 1919), par. 26.

[2] Memorandum on the Setting up of Departmental Councils in the Administrative and Legal Departments of the Civil Service (1919), par. 1.

scheme for the re-classification of the administrative executive, and clerical grades of civil servants, and their rates of pay ; arranged a system by which cost of living increases (and decreases) should be controlled ; and provided a set of rules to regulate promotions. The reports of these sub-committees were accepted and their application begun.[1] For some time the Postmaster-General resisted the proposal to include his Department within the Whitley scheme, and consented only after keen agitation by the unions. All the Councils have now dealt with a mass of work, and helped materially to tide Government Departments over the very difficult post-war days.

Early in 1922 the Government began to retire from the position it had taken up with regard to Whitleyism in the Civil Service. The whole machinery, so far as it concerned remuneration, had been planned and built, on the assumption that the final resort to force in case of deadlock would be obviated by agreed arbitration. Since 1917 the Civil Service Arbitration Board had dealt with a great deal of such business, and while it had not always satisfied the " staff " side, its awards had been accepted in the spirit of the scheme. To the " official " side arbitration was probably never welcome, and the clamour for economy in public affairs during 1921–2, provided an opportunity for abolishing the Board. It had cost nearly £4,000 [2] a year—an insignificant item in the adjustment of the wages of over 300,000 workers. Expense was the first reason given for its abolition, but two other more important reasons were put forward, viz. that

[1] Joint Industrial Councils Bulletin, No. 3, September, 1920.
[2] Circular issued by the Joint Committee of Civil Service Staff Organizations, April 26, 1922, par. 4.

the Board was not under the control of the Chancellor of the Exchequer, and that it was a deterrent to the smooth working of the Whitley system.[1] The latter was not justified by experience up to that time. Conciliation work had proceeded, despite the existence of an arbitration body, and there had not been any general tendency, on the workers' side, to press obstinately for arbitration where compromise was possible. The second point, therefore, probably represented the true cause. The Treasury wished, apparently, to recover the veto it had so nobly sacrificed at the altar of peace and co-operation,[2] and owing to the constitution of the Whitley Councils that veto could be virtually recovered by the removal of arbitration.[3] The opposition of the staff associations to this change was unavailing. No arbitration authority has replaced the old Board. There is no longer any means of clearing off disagreements. In the old days grievances accumulated and discontent grew steadily until a partial adjustment, long overdue, was made by a Royal Commission or Select Committee. It is not likely that this will happen to a similar extent in the future, for conciliation has already proved a valuable solvent of difficulties and has done much to make a less antagonistic atmosphere. Yet there must be deadlocks ; the strike is not " readily available " to State servants, and some friction and discontent will remain. The appointment of three members of Parliament to the National Whitley Council con-

[1] Circular issued by the Joint Committee of Civil Service Staff Organizations, April 26, 1922, par. 3.

[2] See p. 140.

[3] Decisions must be agreements and thus the Treasury representatives on a Council could block a decision.

stitutes no real substitute for the Arbitration Board, particularly since it is intended that they shall be members of the party in power. The Arbitration Board had no political flavour. The external members of the National Whitley Council will change with political fortunes, and wage-assessment by political standards is far less desirable, in several ways, than the semi-judicial awards of an arbitration body.

In Government employment generally, however, Joint Industrial Councils have carried the collective bargain a step further. The principle of organization is tacitly acknowledged by the setting up of such organizations. Representatives on the workers' side of the Councils are drawn from the trade unions concerned. This has meant that industrial or professional organization has been practically forced upon workers who, in some departments, have been least ready to join with their fellows. In its earliest phases the Whitley Council in Civil Service affairs seemed likely to help in the solution of the problem of dual control. There appeared a possibility that the State might be able to separate its function as employer from its character as sovereign. The Ministerial head of a Department was still left responsible to Parliament in matters of policy, and he remained able to refuse terms offered by the workers. Later experience has shown the difficulties which lie in the way of cutting administration adrift from politics, and has set forth more clearly the dangers which such a course would involve. A Parliamentary pronouncement in a State wages dispute is evidently accepted at present very much in the same spirit as an arbitration award, though it seeks generally to lay down lines of policy rather than to work out details. In this respect alone, therefore, there is ample work for conciliation bodies, and the Councils have undoubtedly removed many causes of friction. They may help also to remove the confusion of thought which assumes that State employment rests on bases different from those of private employment, because the State is also sovereign. The need of the State for industrial security in time of emergency seems in no way imperilled by the new arrangements, for with closer understanding should come readier co-operation ; and if that hope failed, special legislation, such as the war brought, would achieve what conciliation failed to produce.

NOTE.—A Parliamentary agitation by the Civil Service Confederation this year (1923) has resulted in the appointment, by the Chancellor of the Exchequer, of a joint committee to consider the question of arbitration. It seems probable that some form of arbitration to deal with Civil Service wages questions will again be provided.

THE METHODS OF FOREIGN GOVERNMENTS

THE wage-systems of foreign Governments can have no detailed examination here, but in the brief survey which is possible some interesting facts may be found. As might be expected, wage conditions reflect in a surprising degree the stage of political development at which a nation has arrived. Austria, for instance, had made trade union activity in the public services ineffective, before the war, not by legislative but by administrative action. Germany had achieved a similar end by personal surveillance. Australia, at the opposite end of the scale, had admitted collective bargaining in full, and had interposed compulsory arbitration between the failure to agree and the resort to a trial of strength.

In practically all cases respect for the personality of the worker is to be found. Security of tenure and the prospect of a pension are granted to Government employees in nearly all civilized nations, but in the most advanced communities the idea of automatic progression of pay along fixed incremental scales has given way to a system by which the efficiency and industry of the worker are scrutinized periodically, and his advancement regulated accordingly. The movement of the English Civil Service in this direction has already been noted as of post-war date.[1]   In

[1] Chap. IV, p. 128.

New South Wales systematic regrading quinquenially was instituted in 1910,[1] and in Victoria the practice of reclassifying school teachers every three years was adopted soon after.[2] Methods of this sort, if they needed justification, could be supported by the contention that in Australia, since the introduction of compulsory arbitration, wages have been graded upwards, in a ratio determined by demand and supply, but based, for unskilled labour, upon what Mr. Justice Higgins calls the " human needs of labour." This has been declared by the President of the Australian Court of Conciliation and Arbitration to be the basis of his awards.[3] He adopted, in fixing the wages for unskilled workers, " the normal needs of the average employee, regarded as a human being living in a civilized community." [4] Above this figure the normal proportions have been maintained between different grades of labour. Thus the wages of Government workers in Australia have been good, and the right to demand good service in return is a natural corollary. In some states there has been reason to suspect that the wages have been too good. State-owned railways appear to have caused most trouble in this respect, and charges of inefficient service, owing to political wire-pulling, are not unknown.[5] Apart from the awards of arbitration, however, the

---

[1] Answer to questionnaire, First Appendix to Fourth Report Royal Commission on Civil Service (Cd. 7339 of 1914), p. 190.

[2] *Ibid.*, p. 194.

[3] Higgins: " A New Province for Law and Order " (" Harvard Law Review," November, 1915).

[4] *Ibid.*

[5] Memorandum prepared by Intelligence Division of Ministry of Labour, November, 1919: " Trade Unions in Nationalized Industries," p. 9.

Australian States have frequently had regard to the "living wage." Probationary candidates for the Civil Service of Queensland in 1913 were given a salary of £50, with an addition of £20 if they were employed in a place where they could not live with their parents.[1] Since the adoption of arbitration for the Commonwealth employees, Parliamentary control has been safeguarded by the provision, in the Act of 1911, that awards shall be laid on the table of the House of Parliament for 30 days after their issue, and may be disapproved by Parliament during that period.   If no action is taken within that time they become operative.[2]

Most European countries have lagged far behind this ideal.   Few have succeeded in preventing trade unionism from invading the State service, from which fact it might be assumed that wages had resulted from collective bargaining. This is probably not true, since the right to strike is generally withheld.   In France, Article 126 of the Penal Code makes a strike of public servants a criminal offence, though, according to a recent statement, conditions of employment on the railways are agreed "between the political and administrative personnel."[3] It is clear from the action of the French Government in calling up railway strikers to the colours that the ultimate authority in the fixing of terms and enforcing their acceptance is with the employer.

Since 1908, when a general strike took place on

[1] Answer to questionnaire, First Appendix to Fourth Report, Royal Commission on Civil Service (Cd. 7339 of 1914), p. 193.   The starting wage of assistant clerks in England at that time was £45.

[2] Ministry of Labour Memorandum, "Trade Unions in Nationalized Industries," p. 10.

[3] *Ibid.*, p. 11.

the Dutch railways, Holland has made it a criminal offence for State employees to strike or to conspire to bring about a strike. Italy adopted the same course in 1889, and has further protected itself, in the matter of State railways, by requiring, under a law of 1906, that all private railway undertakings shall draw up, and submit to the Ministry of Public Works, disciplinary rules similar to those applied in the service of the State railways, and consequently including penalties for striking.[1]

Germany and Austria, before the war, had no legislative prohibition of strikes in Government service, yet each country in its own way took effective steps to prevent the use of this weapon by the workers. Austria achieved this by requiring that the rules and by-laws of such trade unions should be submitted to the authorities. If they were found to be " dangerous to the State " a society could be dissolved, and several unions of public officials were suppressed in this way by the judgment of the Supreme Court.[2] It was provided also that twenty-four hours' notice of any trade union meeting must be given, in order that a representative of the Government might attend.

In Germany a worker's right to join a trade union was contingent upon the approval of the union by his superiors. This was not avowed, but was made a practice before the war. The State railways, too, were staffed, as far as possible, with ex-N.C.O's.— a class least likely to favour trade unionism and most readily amenable to discipline.[3]

While these facts are not direct evidence as to

[1] Ministry of Labour Memorandum, " Trade Unions in Nationalized Industries," p. 56.
[2] *Ibid.*, pp. 59 and 60.
[3] *Ibid.*, p. 63.

wage-fixing they indicate the limitations placed upon collective bargaining, while the strikes which have taken place in Government services on the Continent prove the existence of grievances.   That the services offer a great attraction to workers there can be no doubt, and it seems possible that in some cases advantage has been taken of this to keep wage-rates down.   On this subject the following statement as to Belgium, where strikes are also punishable by fine or imprisonment, is significant :   " The absence of strikes on the Belgian railways is stated to be due to the fact that employment on the railways is more and more sought after.   Men, who would earn higher wages in other vocations, enter the service of the railway because of its stability, the prospect of a pension, and on account of the consideration which they enjoy as public servants." [1]   In Belgium, therefore, the competition for places enables the State to pay lower wages than those paid outside.   In France, too, admission to the service of the State is a privilege for which some payment must be made. In certain departments, such as that of *Contributions Directes*, candidates have to serve on probation for two years without any remuneration, and are then started on a very low salary.[2]   Private means are necessary for persons holding appointments in the diplomatic and consular services, for which no candidate is accepted on probation until he has produced evidence that he has sufficient means to maintain himself for two years.[3]

[1] Ministry of Labour Memorandum, " Trade Unions in Nationalized Industries," p. 49.

[2] Answer to questionnaire, First Appendix to Fourth Report, Royal Commission on Civil Service (Cd. 7339 of 1914), p. 168.

[3] *Ibid.*

Most of these Governments employ a large number of women. The number in France in 1913 was 155,300,[1] including a great many teachers. Generally the female officers are paid on a lower scale than men. The best-paid women servants in France before the war were the teachers, whose scales were about one-tenth less than those of men.[2] The women employed by the Netherlands Government in the Departments of Posts, Telegraphs, and Justice, and in the State Insurance Bank, received the same scales as men.[3] In New South Wales and Victoria the wages of women servants of the State were generally 25 per cent. below those for men of similar grades.[4] It is interesting that in most countries female service is estimated as of lower value than corresponding service by men. In England the reason adduced for this difference has generally been that the " market rate " settled the ratio, though there has been some acknowledgment recently, under the influence of living-wage theories, of the need to pay a " family wage " to men. In view of this, it is particularly interesting that Australia, with its Labour Governments and its humanitarian basis for wage-rates, should retain the distinction ; for only in certain instances can it now be shown that the output of women workers is seriously below that of men doing similar work, and the persistence of the difference in wages, under conditions such as those of Australia, directs attention to the fundamental difference between the minimum supply prices of male and female labour. It is clear that the supply price of women's labour is generally determined simply by

[1] Answer to questionnaire. First Appendix to Fourth Report, Royal Commission on Civil Service (Cd. 7339 of 1914), p. 169.
[2] *Ibid.*, p. 168.   [3] *Ibid.*, pp. 172–81.   [4] *Ibid.*, pp. 189 and 194.

the needs of an individual, while that of men's labour is based upon the needs of a family.

In considering the wages of most of these Governments, the chief impression gained is that wage-fixing was a matter which demanded little energy or ingenuity, that it was looked upon as a matter which would right itself almost automatically. Before the war no country except Australia could boast machinery for adjusting wages to changing conditions, or for dealing with claims made by the workers. Yet in many cases movement resulted only from pressure by employees or by shortage of supply. A prominent example of this is to be found in the State services of the United States of America. It is claimed that when wage scales for Government employment were set after the Civil War they were " liberal as compared both with the cost of living and the prevailing wages and salaries outside of Government service." [1] That ended the matter as far as voluntary attention to the subject was concerned, and as a recent writer has said : " The Government appeared to feel that the matter was done with for ever and took no further steps except when, in some particular group or division, conditions arose which forced action." [2] The United States Government had meant well, and as soon as war conditions brought changes in the cost of living prominently before its notice showed its approval of the principle of maintaining real wages,[3] but it had never stopped to consider whether real wages had

---

[1] " Monthly Labour Review " (U.S.A.), Vol. X, No. 6. Article on " The Government's Wage Policy," p. 19.

[2] *Ibid.*

[3] This is seen in the setting up of the National War Labour Board, the Macy Board for shipyards, and the legislation as to railway wages.

changed without the upheaval of a great war. That they had changed, and that the Government had paid no attention to such movements until pressed, may be seen from some of the following facts. During the period 1893–1919, the average salary of all Government workers, in the district of Columbia, advanced from 1,096 dollars to 1,321 dollars, whereas if salaries had followed the rise in the cost of living during that time, it would have risen to 2,839 dollars.[1] The fall in real wages was even more remarkable in a small group of workers. The average salary of the assistants in the reading room and catalogue divisions of the Library of Congress fell from 1,200 dollars in 1897 to 982 dollars in 1919, though it should have risen to 3,396 dollars.[2] Proof that pressure alone could bring changes is afforded by the fact that while most wages were stationary during this period, those of compositors and pressmen were advanced to the trade union scale, because the Government was " obliged to meet strong outside competition " and could see no other way " of keeping up the force in the Government Printing Office." [3] As might be expected the grades of skilled labour were much more ready for trade union organization than those of the clerical, scientific, and technical services, and the advances secured by the former were considerably higher than those of the professional class.[4] One or both of two influences, then, have generally decided movements in the wages of the United States services—labour agitation and the

---

[1] " Monthly Labour Review " (U.S.A.), Vol. X, No. 6. Article on " The Government's Wage Policy," Table on p. 21.
[2] *Ibid.*, p. 23.
[3] *Ibid.*, p. 28.
[4] *Ibid.*, p. 30.

competition of private enterprise.   Where the elements of monopoly existed the tendency to stagnation was most accentuated.   Here is the conclusion arrived at by an investigator : " The Government raises salaries only when it is forced to do so in order to keep its employees, and then only so far as will enable it to withstand outside competition.   When there is no such competition, as, for instance, when the Government is the only employer for some line of scientific or technical work and there is therefore little chance for the worker outside, salaries tend to remain stationary, or are advanced slowly and uncertainly to an extent which is wholly insufficient to meet the increase in the cost of living." [1]

Thus, in the United States, as in England, outside wage-rates have exerted a considerable influence, and the same difficulty of meeting the monopolist employer of labour on fair terms has been experienced.   The temptation to evade scientific examination and adjustment of wages, where the Government is the only employer, is seen to be extremely powerful and may be combated, apparently only by very determined pressure, such as postal workers employed in England or by the popular acceptance of a living-wage creed, as in the Commonwealth of Australia.   In European countries collective bargaining has not been allowed to reach its full development, and, clearly, wages have resulted from the relations of supply to demand.   The ideal of continuity and provision for old age has been aimed at in most cases, but the tendency throughout Europe has been to make these privileges an excuse for not paying the market rate of wages, rather than

[1] " Monthly Labour Review " (U.S.A.), Vol. X, No. 6. Article on " The Government's Wage Policy," p. 30.

the subject of scientific assessment in respect of which definite deductions from wages are to be made. Australia has taken this question in hand, and for the lower grades of State workers pension deductions, generally not exceeding 4 per cent are made.

In all cases it is clear that Governments do not set up standards which are generally higher than those maintained by various methods in private industry. Governments, as employers of labour, have a marked inclination to follow, slowly, the conditions arrived at in ordinary employment rather than to cut new lines for themselves.   Not often do they attempt to lead. More often, in democratic countries, they are content to regard outside conditions as interpreting the will of the nation and to follow that will, in industrial affairs, as they usually follow it in legislative matters. Similarly, as most legislation is conceded after popular demand, so changes in labour conditions have needed agitation.   Politically, one assumes, things are all right when noisy criticism is not forthcoming.   That view of the industrial situation has not been justified in the past because organization has been generally discouraged and absolute collective bargaining has been refused, with the result that agitation has not been carried on and wages have suffered.

Government service throughout the world is attractive, and competition for admission is becoming more keen, yet the realization, on the part of the workers, that they may not rely upon the altruism of their employers or even upon their sense of justice is gaining strength.   Hence arises a determination to press for adjustment, which almost invariably traverses the lines of private enterprise and so strengthens the existing tendency of Governments to be satisfied with outside standards, and to abandon any incipient desire to approach the question from a different angle. It is chiefly the fault of the Governments that this is so. Some of them started well, and assumed that the work was finished when wage scales had once been fixed, tabulated, and filed for reference. By the time that adjustment was overdue workers found ready to hand useful comparisons outside, and naturally adopted them. Most Governments, through having no policy, have found themselves gradually saddled, almost in spite of themselves, with the policy existing in private employment, and a few ill-defined additions.

CHAPTER VI

CONCLUSIONS

THE most prominent feature which the present inquiry reveals is the persistent influence of demand and supply in the fixing of Government wages. For the broad outlines this is naturally to be expected, but the weakening of those devices which tone down the harshness of its results is a surprising development. It is not, as far as Great Britain is concerned, a deliberate abandonment of the principle of respecting the personality of the worker so much as a half-unconscious lowering of standards under the pressure of economy, and because of the closer contact with private business and ordinary outside labour. Perhaps there was a good underlying reason—never convincingly expressed, possibly only partially realized—for the opposition of certain employing Departments to the organization of their workers on the lines of ordinary trade unions. It may be that the Admiralty knew that touch with the rest of the industrial world would necessarily mean the adoption of outside standards by the workers. It is true that the workers themselves have done much to demolish the old idea of State employment, with its distinctive features and aims. It is also true that the workers' assault would not have been made if State employment had attained its original ideal. That ideal throughout has been vague and unavowed. Yet the early history of State wages gives evidence of a real attempt to treat the workers as something more than " a mere tenement for so much labour." Generally the State employee had constant work, he was secure for the whole of his life, he was given medical attention when necessary, with pay during illness, and he had a pension to look forward to. When important changes in methods of work came along, the Government sought to retain the men whose old skill was no longer of use and to teach them some part of the new processes. Wages as a whole were fixed, not perhaps on generous lines, but at least on scales which were a fair reflex of demand and supply, and they remained unaltered by the temporary variations of boom or slump.

That condition endured until Government undertakings began to assume fairly large proportions. Then, for whatever reasons, the spirit of economy gripped the Treasury and communicated itself to most Departments. Several influences made the Treasury's position unenviable during this period. Prices had been rising throughout the second half of last century. The standard of comfort had risen as the trade union movement gained strength. The standards of civilization had advanced, bringing new and expensive duties for the State to perform. As in the United States, adjustment of wages had been neglected until it was clamoured for. Adjustments long overdue, consequently, involved heavy costs. The new lines of State service came crowding with their high expenses. Not only did the wages of the individual employee grow, but also the total of employees grew enormously. The Treasury found its wage-bill swelling tremendously, and, quite naturally, it gasped.

Economy seemed to be imperative, and since, in the new circumstances, economy could not be avowedly ruthless, the Treasury turned to the most excusable example—outside industry.

Then started the abridging of what had the flavour of an idealist scheme. Not only was there a weakening of all the influences which aimed at securing the well-being of the worker, but by various devices actual wage-rates were cut. Apparently the Treasury was either unable to appreciate the special points of this ideal for Government employment, or was unable to afford to retain them. Suitable wage-bases were not sought. With the admission of " commercial " principles comparisons with wages in " commercial " undertakings were looked for. Contractors did much work similar to that done in Government establishments, and the example of outside industry became too obtrusive—for the Treasury when it examined its wage-bill and then for the workers when they found their own wages being manipulated.

If such a special system of wage fixing were feasible it might have been expected to succeed in Government employment. The pressure experienced in capitalist enterprise and competition had not to be met. A corresponding pressure crept in when the Treasury tightened its control on expenditure—a pressure deriving its strongest characteristics from purely commercial standards. The record of the Treasury on wage matters has not been a good one. It has interpreted" model employer " as " average employer." It has been content that its wage-rates should be " not less favourable " than those in private employment. Its whole attitude is summed up by the following opinion of Mr. Sidney Webb : " It is just because the Treasury control has been exclusively directed to cutting down expenditure, that is, to parsimony—never once, it is believed, has the Treasury ever pressed on a Department an increase of expenditure by means of which a more than proportionate increase of efficiency could be obtained —which is what the House of Commons nowadays most desires, that the Treasury control has broken down." [1] If the last part of that quotation is true, it means that the Treasury has exercised the prerogative in wage fixing with so little control that it failed entirely to reflect the wishes of Parliament. Yet even the attempt of the House of Commons to set wage definitions has failed. The Fair Wages Clause, as applied to Government Departments, has proved most unsatisfactory, partly because this movement sought to prescribe the same rule of thumb for two different sets of industrial conditions—private and State.

Both Treasury and House of Commons have misunderstood the spirit which seemed, almost involuntarily, to be striving for expression in State service. Both have assumed that the State's system of wages could be improved only by assimilating it to that of private employment. If the original design had been retained intact, and if the temptation to manipulate wages had been resisted, a model system would have been set up, embodying ideals rarely found in private business. It is not clear that conditions ever came very near to achieving the ideal, but evidently the spirit was there in the earlier days. The Treasury gave way to the influence of commercial example ; the House of Com-

---

[1] Letter in reply to questionnaire ; published in Ninth Report, Committee on National Expenditure (1918), p. 27.

mons to the agitation which that departure evoked from the workers. Both policies were of similar intent; aimed from different angles, at stripping State wages of their distinctiveness and at adapting them to private standards ; aimed at removing ethical considerations and substituting the pure economics of capitalist enterprise. Out of this new attitude has arisen most of the evils of capitalist employment—rate-cutting, in the dockyards by means of poorly paid " skilled labourers " ; in the Post Office by the excessive use of cheap auxiliary labour and the setting up of unfair schedules ; in the Civil Service by the increasing employment of temporary clerks. Speeding-up appeared in the piecework methods of the War Office ; advantage of special conditions was taken by the Post Office in its dealings with rural postmen ; no adjustment of real wages took place without pressure from the workers ; and, all round, the " establishment " rule became lax. The old ideal was not entirely abandoned. Just after the war it seemed likely to take a new lease of life, though its rehabilitation is made the more difficult because the workers have met these grievances, very naturally, with the adoption of commercial standards for the purpose of comparison on their side.

The unexpressed ideal of Government wages seems to have been concerned rather with the form than the amount of remuneration. It must be readily admitted that no justification could exist for the paying of better rates than those paid for similar work outside. That would mean creating a privileged class. " Fair " wages, therefore, may be assumed to be those arrived at by collective bargaining, in which both sides are well organized. This must decide the value of labour,

since the Government has been unable to find any
substitute for supply and demand owing to the
absence of an accepted ethical principle. The value
of labour can be separated from the form of its
remuneration, and it is in this respect that Government
wages tended to diverge from the normal commercial
practice. A system which offered security, recognized
the status of the worker, and gave him something to
hope for in the nature of increments and a pension, is a
distinct improvement on the hourly or weekly rate of
private employment. In the long run it does not appear
to be quite as economical, which probably accounts
for its comparative failure or the frequent lapses.

The resort to ordinary methods of wage fixing has
been made almost complete since the war. Collective
bargaining is acknowledged and practised, as it must
inevitably have been whenever confidence in the
justice and fairness of the employers broke down.
The Government has had to separate its functions of
sovereign and employer and to deal with workers in
the typical industrial fashion. It is not clear, however,
whether this could have been avoided. Possibly the
workers would have been slower to turn to the
standards of the outside world if the pruning knife
had not been used so readily on their wages. On the
other hand, the experience of the Australian Governments suggests that, in the most favourable
circumstances, organized bargaining is essential. Nor
is it certain that generous and frank treatment alone
will produce a return of sustained high endeavour
in the workers. This is an important point, for if
good wages do not bring high efficiency, economic
pressure must, in the long run, force a readjustment.
The assurance of continuity in Government employ-

ment constitutes one of its greatest difficulties in this respect. The fear of dismissal may not be held over the worker who fails to give his best. The stopping of an increment may have some effect, but can only be partial; and the path of promotion has not been sufficiently unencumbered in the past to form a powerful incentive.

Constitutionally, the change of wage-policy is important. The separation of governmental functions has taken place without any real detraction from the authority or even the dignity of the Government and its Departments. Ministerial responsibility and Treasury control remain, the latter without its offensive autocracy and aloofness. The reins are still held ultimately by Parliament, and the removal of wage questions from the political to the industrial sphere renders less formidable the danger of political pressure of the type exerted, in the early years of this century, by postal officials. Those who feared that industrial democracy in Government service would imperil the sovereignty of the political democracy have found no justification for their fears in recent developments.

A new problem remains, however. Wages in Government service have become very similar to those of private industry. The privileges have become appendages instead of the integral items which they used to be. Output is being measured and set alongside the pay given for it. The standards are becoming increasingly commercial, and private firms are ready to carry out much of the work for which the State now employs labour direct. War-time experience raises the question as to whether the old manufacturing establishments of the State are

necessary in their old form. The possibility of
quickly adapting the private concerns of the nation
to the production of the munitions and stores needed
in war-time has been amply proved, and the advocacy
of maintaining a large reserve of potential producing
power in the hands of the State has lost much of its
force. If the tendency to reduce some of the Government establishments—already foreshadowed in the
report of the Committee on National Expenditure,
1922—develops, it will probably be found that the
assimilation of Government wages to outside standards
will aid the movement. Standing charges will be
avoided, and the wage-systems of State concerns will
be hardly more worth conserving than those secured
to workers in private employ by the Fair Wages Clause
of Government contracts.

The model which Government employment was
intended to set has become strangely similar to the
average type. Yet the Service, in all its branches,
remains extraordinarily popular with the wage-earning
classes. Here, perhaps, is contained the greatest
lesson which State wages have to teach. Security
and regularity are an irresistible attraction to the
vast mass of workers. Risk, with the possibility of
high gain, is chosen by the few only ; and, for the rest,
wages may readily enough include debit items in
respect of absence of anxiety and the prospect of a
comfortable old age. State wage-systems have not,
however, solved the other side of the problem. They
have not shown how effort may be ensured when no
danger of poverty exists and when the spur of high
possibilities does not enter. It would seem that the
enduring nature of such problems proves the im-
possibility of finding a solution in the " mechanics "

of wage fixing, and points to the neglect of the purely moral considerations on both sides.

The position of the Government as an employer is certainly a peculiar one. The public will allow wages to be fixed in private employment by pure bargaining, but when the Government takes up the question the application of some moral principle is expected. Our economic system leaves the problem of valuation, which is the central point, to supply and demand, and thus offers no help to the legislator or administrator. As a matter, largely, of Parliamentary technique he has to formulate an ethical and political principle by reference to which his administration can be justified. The advance of industrial organization among the workers has intensified this difficulty, raising new criticism of principles and emphasizing afresh the indefiniteness of moral concepts and the enduring conflict between ethical and economic principles.

APPENDIX A

TRADE UNION FIGHT AGAINST ADMIRALTY'S "SKILLED LABOURER" SYSTEM.

THE following are extracts from the reports of the Parliamentary Committee of the Trades Union Congress. They describe the interviews of deputations with successive First Lords :—

Report, Parliamentary Committee, March, 1908.

Deputation to First Lord of Admiralty (Lord Tweedmouth).

Mr. D. C. Cummings (Boilermakers) said that they had conclusively shown in the past that the wages of ironworkers in the shipyards were at least 20 to 25 per cent. below those paid in the private yards of the country for time workers, and probably 40 to 50 per cent. for pieceworkers. He urged that the rates of men employed upon ironwork in His Majesty's dockyards should be put upon an equal footing with those of the private yards, and that they should be apprenticed to their various callings.

Mr. W. Mosses (Patternmakers) said objection was made to the premium bonus system being employed in the Admiralty works. The system was dishonest.

Lord Tweedmouth, in reply, said he could not hold out a very great deal of hope of a great change in those matters. The skilled labourer was a very important element of our dockyard organization, and the work in the dockyards was very different from that in the private yards. Their desire was to keep the men continually at work, and if a man could do work of varying sorts they were obliged to adopt a system differing from the one in vogue in the private yards. It was for the good of the dockyard and for the good of the men themselves. These now had permanent employment, but if the present system was discontinued they would have to be continually discharging men, in order that particular work might be carried on by these special tradesmen. They would thus be having continual changes in the staff which would be very unsatisfactory. He clung to the system of employing the skilled labourer and giving him higher pay when he was doing special work ; when the work was done he dropped back to the ordinary scale of pay, and at any rate he got a living when not employed on special work. Therefore he could not hold out hope that they were going to give up the system.

As to the premium bonus system, he thought that had been put forward rather from an exaggerated point of view. As a matter of fact there were altogether in the employment of the dockyards about 28,000 or 29,000 men, and those who were employed on the premium bonus system were on the average only about 750. The system was only used in cases of particular work on which only a very few men could be employed. It was generally work which was difficult, arduous, and causing a considerable amount of inconvenience, and it was a good thing to hold out to the men some sort of inducement to " stick " to their work. They got extra pay for doing better and quicker work. At Chatham the wages of the men working under the system amounted to £426 6s. 7d. while their absolute earnings were £517 3s. 5d. That was proof that the men did not lose by it. They wanted to avoid "overtime." The premium bonus system was a method by which overtime was reduced, and he could not hold out hope that the system would be dropped.[1] He did not mean to say by that that it would be used to a great extent, but that they would use it for the particular work for which they had found it useful. They found that the men liked the system very much and were glad to be working under it. He did not think it led to un-employment—it only gave a useful incitement. It held out great inducement to men who perhaps might be backward to exert themselves under this system.

Eighth Quarterly Report, Parliamentary Committee, March, 1911.

Deputation to First Lord of Admiralty, February 9.

Mr. J. Hill (Boilermakers), referred to the following Resolution :

"That this Congress condemns the system obtaining in the Royal Dockyards of putting handy men, called 'skilled labourers,' at a compara-tively low rate of wages, to do the work which is done by duly apprenticed tradesmen in private shipyards ; and calls upon the Government to give direct Labour Repre-sentation on the Fair Wages Inter-Depart-mental Committee." . . .

In the building of royal warships we complain that pinching, shearing, bending, riveting and caulking,

---

[1] On overtime, an employer pays at *more* than the normal rate for extra work ; under premium bonus systems, at *less* than the normal rate.

all of which is considered to be skilled work in other
dockyards—even in the building of a tramp it is paid
for as skilled work—is regarded as labourers' work.
You take on boys at 6s. per week, rising until at the
age of 20 they may have the handsome maximum
of 16s. ; and at the end of the time, having served
their apprenticeship they are not classed as tradesmen
but as skilled labourers. These men may rise to what
I understand is about the average of 26s. per week,
and in the very dim future they may even get to the
higher maximum of 28s. 6d. We contend that this
system makes it impossible for these men to become
skilled craftsmen, after having given their lives to
the work ; it takes them into a blind alley from
which there is no outlet, and there will be none unless
you alter the system. These men have no voice,
except in the petitions,[1] in connexion with the fixing
of the prices of the various jobs they are put to from
time to time. . . .

In the private yards these men have the fullest
possible recognition. They are looked upon as
tradesmen and classed as such. Their wages are at
least 10s. per week higher than the wages paid to
your " skilled labourers." The great bulk of the
work is performed at piece rates and considerably
higher wages are earned. . . .

Last year you issued a statement and intimated
that an advance in the maximum rates would be
given. Establishment men were to be increased from
26s. to 28s. 6d. and the hired men's maximum from
28s. to 30s. We welcomed that at the time and said
it was a step in the right direction, but we have
had letters from the various dockyards complaining

---

[1] The " petitions " system is described in Chap. II, pp. 28–34.

bitterly about the restrictions that have been put on this advanced maximum. You say in your notes that the new rates of pay will be regarded as special, and will be awarded to the more limited number of skilled men who are using tools as responsible workmen. You notice that they must be responsible workmen actually using tools on the skilled work in the building of battleships, and even of these there is only to be a limited number. The result has been that, so far, very few have been able to obtain the advance.

Mr. J. Jenkins: . . . At one time—I am speaking of the commencement of the iron and steel shipbuilding in the dockyards—the trade I represent did the whole of the work now referred to in this resolution. The director of the dockyards will know that the shipwrights did the caulking, the riveting and everything in the construction of the ship. But the shipwrights were regarded as very skilled craftsmen and they received, notwithstanding that they were doing the riveting and caulking, the higher rate of pay. But the Admiralty said: "You relax your muscles and we will use your brains." Then they introduced what you are pleased to call the "skilled labourer." . . . When this change came about you said to the skilled labourer class : "Now we are going to raise you a little above your fellows. When you were in the boatswain's gang you were receiving 21s., now we are going to graduate you up to 28s., thus making the average wage 25s." Of course you were good enough last year to raise the maximum to 30s., but few of the men have been able to obtain the increase. In fact, when I presented the petition a few months ago on behalf of the drillers, I found that not one in 70 had received the higher rate, and only one received

29s. Any man studying the Navy Estimates will appreciate the difference in the volume of trade you send outside as compared with what is done in the dockyards. You have to pay 36s. or 39s. to the men outside, and yet in your own dockyards men are working for 23s. or 28s., or an average of 25s. per week. These are plain facts. You might urge that the dockyards have got the 48 hours, but many places outside also work the 48-hour week, although we may take the average to be 52 hours. Men in the dockyards, however, do not work by the hour, but by the day. In my own district we work 46 hours, and if we were working on Government work we should do no more and be receiving a higher rate of pay. To a great extent, I know that men in the dockyards are employed more regularly than those outside. But it is a fact that on the Clyde there is as much work as it will be possible to find men for during the next three years. But there are fluctuations of work even in the dockyards, and in the year 1904 or 1905 we had some 3,000 men discharged from the dockyards, although they had been there a number of years. You may also suggest that this class of men has graduated from labourers. But no one would suggest that they are in any way inferior to the men employed. They must be made highly skilled, whether by your own instructors in the dockyards or elsewhere.

The boatswain's gang has been referred to. Sometimes you have to transfer men to the boatswain's gang because you have not enough work for them. They have been employed for years and years and now will go back to the boatswain's gang because it pays you far better to retain them in your employment, and in the whole of the dockyards there is plenty of work for this purpose. But supposing these men do go back to the boatswain's gang I should not complain so long as they received a proper rate of pay while they were working as mechanics. The percentage of men employed in the dockyards receiving a pension is very small indeed. It is not 33⅓ per cent. They have fallen far below that, but recently, I know, you have considerably extended the scheme.

Reply of First Lord (McKenna).

. . . Let me take the last case first. Mr. Jenkins is a very skilled rhetorician ; he puts his case in the best possible way. But I am bound in replying to point out to you that his case is a rhetorical case more than a real one. He knows what my reply is and therefore he anticipates it. He says : " I know it will be said that these men are employed first in one trade and then in another ; you do not want to dismiss them and therefore you keep them on and adopt the skilled labourer system instead of having tradesmen like other firms." And then he says : " I know men who are employed for years doing the same work." We have just upon 10,000 skilled labourers in our employ, and of the total how many men does he know who have been employed for years on one branch of the shipbuilding business ? I have been round the dockyards and have heard their cases and have received petitions, and I have found here and there, it is quite true, men who have been employed at the same work for a considerable time. But of the 10,000 the overwhelming majority are men employed in one trade to-day and in another to-morrow. That is the case. I will admit straight away that you have got an argumentative grievance. I understand it, appreciate and admit it ; and I can put it almost as well as you can. But I can only remedy that argumentative grievance by inflicting a real hardship upon the men. If we dismiss a man in a dockyard then there is, generally speaking, no other employment in the town to which he can turn. At Portsmouth, Chatham, Devonport, there is no other industry and they have to break up their homes and leave if we dismiss them. They cannot go to another firm. Our conditions of employment are quite different to the conditions existing in Newcastle, on the Tyne, where they can go from one job to another. When a ship is being built we employ thousands of men on a given class of work and so on. If we employed tradesmen used to one class of work only, as a tradesman would be, we should have to dismiss our riveters and other classes of workmen when we do not require them, and dismiss other classes of workmen in the same way. Thus in our dockyard towns there would be a fluctuating population ; none of them would be as well off as—although individuals might be drawing higher wages for a limited period—the men who are employed in the dockyards now. But mark the consequence of this. It is quite true that when one of our skilled labourers is doing riveting work he must be doing work of the same kind as that performed by a skilled tradesman in the shipbuilding trade outside. Yes, but he is not a skilled tradesman, and he is not always engaged on riveting work, and has not got the skill which is derived from exclusive employment in one trade only. He is working at one trade to-day and another to-morrow. If I employ none but skilled tradesmen, I must dismiss them when I do not want them. As to my skilled labourers, I can employ them to-morrow on something else, and thus avoid the necessity for getting rid of them.   Now which is the better plan ?   I am dealing now, not with the argumentative case, which I admit, but with the real hardship which would affect the men.   Which is the better—that I should keep them in continuous employment as far as I can, and as I do, as you know, at Chatham, or dismiss large numbers of men, break up their homes, and send them away ?   It is obvious that in order to satisfy you on the argumentative case, I must inflict a real handicap on the men. . . .

Well, now another case is raised—the case put by Mr. Hill, which he calls the blind alley case.   He says : " These men are in a blind alley.   The utmost they can rise to is 28s. 6d. per week or 30s. per week on the establishment, and is that a fair prospect for these men ? "   But Mr. Hill is not putting the alternative.   What is the other alternative ?

Mr. Hill : To leave the Service.

First Lord : Leave the Service !   But they are not tradesmen, and you would not let them work as tradesmen.   If these men whose prospects are so unfair that they are in a blind alley in the Government service were thrown out of work what chance would they have of securing employment up North as tradesmen ?

Mr. Hill : It is not because they are not skilled tradesmen, but because they have never earned enough money to join the society, that they would not be allowed to work.

First Lord : Oh, no ; that is not the ground on which they fail to satisfy you.   They are not trained as tradesmen and therefore you would not admit them.   The real fact of the matter is that these men are in better employment with us than ever they would get outside.

Mr. Hill : Some of them are our members now.

Mr. Jenkins : The men in your dockyards are in our union, and they are receiving the same money as is paid outside.

First Lord : But I still say that the great bulk of these men could not get work outside. That is my main argument, and I think Mr. Hill would agree with me. These men have failed to satisfy the conditions that skilled tradesmen have to satisfy. But is it a blind alley after all ? First, there is more or less a certainty of work ; secondly, the wages are paid in towns where the cost of living is not high ; and thirdly, they have the chance of getting on the establishment with a situation for life and they are subject to the pension provisions. Besides, the rates of pay do not cover the whole of their possible earnings. So that, taking their conditions all round, I must reply that although I do get in the course of the petitions from the dockyards complaints from individuals—very often it is a claim that they would like a higher rate of wages : that is a common failure of humanity which we all share—I have not found anything in the nature of general dissatisfaction on the part of the skilled labourers as a class.

Eleventh Quarterly Report, March, 1912. (*February* 16*th,* 1912).

Deputation to Dr. Macnamara.

Mr. Hill spoke on the following resolution, passed by the Newcastle Congress :

" That this Congress condemns the system obtaining in the Royal dockyards of classing men as ' skilled labourers ' at a comparatively

low rate of wages who do the work of
skilled craftsmen in private dockyards, and
calls on the Government to class and pay
these men not lower than men employed
on the same work by contractors."

He said : . . . I am talking particularly on behalf
of those who bend, punch, shear, caulk, and fit the
pieces into position on the hulk of the ships in the
Royal dockyards. Despite all the explanation you
have given us in the past years as to why you should
carry on the present system in the dockyards, it has
never at any time appealed to the members of any
society, neither has it ever appealed to the members
of Congress. They have always said unanimously that
the Government, being a model employer, should at
least give conditions and wages equal to the contractors,
whom you insist should observe proper conditions and
wages for similar work outside. It is not only that
higher wages and conditions are given to men on
Government work outside, but higher wages and
conditions and recognition of status are given to these
men on the various tramps that are built in any
shipyard, and should be given at least in the building
of Royal ships. Mr. Churchill's predecessor in office
last year said that these men were not sufficiently
skilled tradesmen. Well, I ask you, is it a good policy
that you should build these ships with anything but
the best labour ? You surely cannot support the
position. There is no necessity in the Royal dockyards to get inefficient labour to build His Majesty's
ships. We may say that the maximum wages are
not at all in accordance with modern practice in
shipbuilding. We know that boys about the age of
14 start from 6s. to 8s. a week, rising to 18s. per week

at the age of 20. Men start from 22s. rising to a maximum of 30s., with a reduction of 1s. 6d. for those who are on the established list for superannuation. In the engineering department you have changed with the times. We have nothing at all to say in regard to the conditions prevailing in the engineering and boilermaking departments. You are quite abreast of the times, and you have introduced the kind of man necessary for the propulsion of ships by steam instead of those that went with wind in the good old days. But in regard to the dockyards you have the same system prevailing as when you built ships of wood, which had to rely on wind and tide. It is not at all understandable to us why there should be a continuity of this old practice and system, this mere recognition of a name in regard to the shipwrights in the Royal dockyards. We have the name of iron shipwrights, but there is nothing in the name. We do say that the men who do the same work as those in outside yards should receive the same wages. Some of our men in private dockyards earn up to 30s. in a day—your maximum week's wages for men at the top of the list. The same possibility of recognition and advancement should be given to the similar class of workers in the dockyards. . . .

I regret the necessity of bringing this question again and again before you, but these men are becoming more and more clamorous in their demands. More and more of them are joining our organization and requesting that they should have the opportunity of going to private dockyards. So far we have refused them the opportunity. We recognize that they have not quite the same reliability because of the practice in the Royal dockyards of putting them in the boatswain's gang occasionally for some little misdemeanour—a practice which is altogether wrong in principle and would not be tolerated by workmen in private yards. I know your argument, sir, that there is more continuity of employment, but we are prepared to take the risk of more casual employment if it should mean that that would be the result. As to the isolation of Royal dockyards, no dockyard is more isolated than the private dockyard in Barrow-in-Furness, but the system we contend for works admirably in Barrow-in-Furness, the employment being more continuous there than in almost any other of our private dockyards. With proper management of the work we believe there could be continuity and a much better time for all these men as skilled craftsmen recognized as you recognize the men in the boilermaking department. So far as we are concerned, and so far as I as a practical man am concerned, I can see no difference between the skill required in a man to build a boiler of any type in your mechanical or engineering department than in the skill required to fit and refit and caulk the hulls of vessels in the dockyards. . . .

Reply by Dr. Macnamara.

. . . Mr. Hill fails to understand this particular classification of skilled labourer which intercepts a labourer from a mechanic. Let me explain if I can what has led to this policy. A dockyard, as the gentlemen here well know, represents a great variety of occupations, some of a special character. If you take a dockyard as a whole, you cannot get a precise counterpart with outside constructors. You have got the engineering and managing department, you have got the electrical management department, you have got the works department, a naval ordnance department, a naval store department, a victualling department, and certain forms of labour attached to a hospital. There is the dockyard with its walls. That being so, it is not at all an impropriety that this special association of a great variety of occupations should call for an organization which might differ from the organization in outside industries. . . .

Now, for a long time past, for many years, the Admiralty, in organizing this particular multifarious association of industries called a dockyard, has had the threefold scheme of the labourer, the skilled labourer, and the mechanic. Mr. Hill rehearsed our real reason for that when he said that the classification of a skilled labourer means a greater continuity of employment for him. That undoubtedly is a fact. We can transfer a skilled labourer from one job to another, and we do ; whereas if he were classified as a tradesmen, the possibility is that at the close of his job he might have to stand off, as is indeed the case to a very considerable extent in the outside yards. Mr. Hill said that men would be prepared to take the risk of that, but there is this to remember. It would be very serious for the mechanics to be put off, because in a dockyard town—although Barrow-in-Furness is similar, I understand, to a dockyard town —a number of classes of mechanics which we employ would find it difficult in the same neighbourhood to get corresponding work outside the docks to that which they have had inside the yards. I think that will be admitted. Therefore in the interests of continuity of employment we have intercepted these skilled labourers.

The resolution speaks of the comparatively low rate of wages. Well, a skilled labourer is a man who has not served an apprenticeship, but has acquired by experience a certain aptitude and responsibility. We turn that to his and to our mutual advantage, and, so far as I can see we turn that to mutual advantage without prejudice to the mechanics. Now his wages were spoken of as comparatively low. If he is established they run from 22s. to 26s. ; if he is hired from 22s. to 28s., and we have recently introduced—and I am very glad that it is so—a special rate of 29s. to 30s. for men doing more responsible work at machinery and other occupations. Over and above that amount these men do a very great deal of piece-work. Their excess of earnings on an average, I may say, run from 25 to 30 per cent above this maximum. I will call that a fair average piecework rate over their ordinary rate. They work eight hours a day, and, as Mr. Thorne has already mentioned, there is no intention on our part that there should be any relinquishment of that rule. If these men are established they have a pension to which, I at once admit, they very largely contribute. If they are hired men, after seven and 15 years' service, should they be stood off on reduction, they are eligible for a gratuity upon a fixed scale.

I am very familiar with the terms of this resolution. It has been before me at the hearing of the workmen's petitions a good many times. As a matter of fact, I have it before me at this moment, as we have under consideration the replies which are to be sent to the petitions sent in by the men in Pembroke, Devonport, Chatham, Sheerness, and Portsmouth. I cannot at this juncture give any undertaking in the matter.

I can, however, assure the members of the deputation that full, careful, and patient consideration shall be given to this frequently repeated petition that is brought to us protesting against our classification of these men as skilled labourers.   I am afraid it is not possible to go beyond that.

Mr. Thorne : May I ask you if you have a system of seniority when you put off men ?

Dr. Macnamara : You mean on reduction ?

Mr. Thorne : Yes.

Dr. Macnamara : There is a general dockyard regulation dealing with the reduction of men.

Mr. Thorne : When you put off the men, do you put them off according to the length of their service ?

Dr. Macnamara : That is a feature of our regulations.

Mr. Jenkins : In connexion with the skilled labourers, you have advanced that certain men have 29s. and 30s. per week.   I know the percentage is very low.   Might I ask that the maximum should operate in every dockyard ?

Dr. Macnamara : Do I understand you to suggest that there are no men on the higher rate in any particular dockyard ?

Mr. Jenkins : There is no man in receipt of 30s. in Pembroke.

Dr. Macnamara : I have got the figures for Pembroke for November and December, 1911.   There are two skilled labourers, iron caulkers, doing skilled labourers' work at 30s. ; six on machines at 30s. These are hired skilled labourers.

.   .   .   .   .   .

Mr. Hill: . . . If anything like Government

conditions were enforced by any outside contractor there would be a stoppage of work.

Dr. Macnamara : I do not press the point, but we have no difficulty in securing men to take up work in the Royal dockyards.

Mr. Hill : That is because we are not taking them away. We could take thousands of your men from the Royal dockyards, and in fact we are considering whether or not it will be advisible to take them. There is a considerable shortage of riveters and caulkers in the private dockyards and shipyards of the country at the present time, and if we decided to take them there would certainly be a shortage of labour then. That will be the only alternative to a satisfactory arrangement being made by the Department.

Dr. Macnamara : I should like to know whether the man who has not served an apprenticeship, who has worked up to a certain measure of adaptability, whether he would be classified as a tradesman from your point of view or as a skilled labourer ?

Mr. Hill : Yes, as a tradesman.

Dr. Macnamara : Although he has not served an apprenticeship ?

Mr. Hill : If he has been working five years at the trade.

Statement of Petitions of Admiralty employees and answers to them (D.30925/14, Admiralty) :—

Employment of Skilled Labourers.

A variety of requests have been made respecting the organization of labour in the Royal dockyards based on the threefold classification of labourer, skilled labourer, and mechanic.

On February 11, 1914, a deputation from the Parliamentary Committee of the Trades Union Congress placed the following resolution of the Congress before the Board :

" That this Congress condemns the system obtaining in the Royal dockyards and other Government factories of classing men as ' skilled labourers ' at a comparatively low rate of wages, who at present are doing similar work to that done by skilled craftsmen in private shipyards, and calls upon the Government to class and pay these men not lower than men employed on the same class of work by contractors. That the Government be requested to institute a system of apprenticeships in Royal dockyards in all trades."

Further, a number of petitioners at the Dockyards have urged that the men engaged on certain classes of work which is now being performed by skilled labourers should be constituted into trades, with the constituents rated and paid as mechanics.

Other requests are to the effect that certain kinds of work should be performed by men who, although not rated as mechanics, should be separately classified with a descriptive name tallying with the type of work instead of by men coming under the general description of skilled labourers.

The requests in question relate mainly to the work of drilling, riveting, iron caulking, machine tool working, and certain operations in connexion with electrical work.

The answer to these various representations is perhaps most fully set forth in the reply which was given by the Parliamentary and Financial Secretary

to the Parliamentary Committee of the Trades Union
Congress as follows :

" In dealing with the first resolution I must remind
you that a Royal dockyard is really not fairly
comparable to a modern shipbuilding or engineering
works. A Royal dockyard is an institution adapted
year by year to serve the ever-growing and ever more
complex requirements of a fleet the units of which
may be in creation, in infancy, in maturity, or in
decay. The dockyards do not say ' Good-bye ' to a
ship when she is completed ; they renew acquaintance
with her from time to time. The dockyards are not
mere factories turning out the finished article. Therefore within the four walls of a Royal dockyard you
get as many departments as there are rooms in a
house, devoted to as many different purposes. In the
first place, there are the constructive and engineering
departments, there are the works' department, electrical department, naval stores department, captain of
the dockyard's department, naval ordnance department, and the victualling department, to say nothing
of repairs, sail lofts, and so on.

" Not merely are there no shipbuilding works in
any way comparable in the immediate districts in
which the Royal dockyards are situated, but I should
doubt very much whether there is any establishment
of any kind, with so many and so varied occupations
within its four walls in any part of the country.

" That being so, the organization of the labour
personnel has to be adapted to meet these complex
demands. And when Mr. Hill says, as he has said
before, with great force, ' Why don't you organize
exactly like a private yard ? ' the first thing I say
is, that you are not comparing like with like.

" In connexion with all these departments there are a great number of miscellaneous jobs which call for a skill beyond the measure of mere carrying and bringing but not up to the skill required from the highly trained mechanic. If we were to adopt the suggestion that there should be only two classes of labour, viz. the mechanic and the unskilled labourer, we should, first of all, be imposing on the dockyards—this is my view—an organization which is quite unsuited to their special needs.

" That is our attitude towards the question from the point of view of those who are entrusted by the nation with the duty of maintaining the Navy in the highest state of efficiency.

" Looking at it from the point of view of our employees—on whose behalf you have spoken so eloquently—the adoption of the suggestion would mean that it would be impossible to give the continuous employment which we can to-day give to the very large number of men who are classed in this intermediate grade of skilled labourer. Then, again, it would abolish the opportunity which our present system gives for deserving men to advance beyond the position of ordinary labourers.

" Let me take the figures. We have in the shipbuilding and engineering departments about 13,400 skilled labourers. We have about 4,600 unskilled labourers at the present time. These men have not been apprenticed. That very possibly has not been their fault. If the unskilled labourers show aptitude we have an opportunity of advancing them beyond mere fetching and carrying jobs. I should say that probably 70 per cent. of our skilled labourers came to us originally as labourers, not more than 30 per cent being recruited from hired boys.

" You speak about the rate he is paid. First of all, in 1905 the unskilled labourer got 20s. a week. He is now getting 23s. in the Home dockyards (22s. at Haulbowline).

" Then, as for skilled labourers. These rates have been increased since 1905 from a scale of 21s. to 27s. to the present scale, which is as follows :

> Probationary rate. . . . 23s.
> Normal scale . . . . . . 24s. to 28s.
> Special rates . . . . . . 29s., 30s., and 31s.

" But that is by no means the end of the skilled labourer's earning capacity. He is engaged as a time worker, and is sure of his time wages ; but in a great many cases he has opportunities for piecework and earns from 25 to 50 per cent. over his time wages for the time he is so employed. The improved rates of pay granted to skilled labourers have, in fact, formed a very considerable part of the cost of the concessions which have been granted since 1905, which comes to about £250,000 annually. As a matter of fact, the rates we are paying now on the numbers we are employing represent an increase in the wage sheet of £250,000, the rises of wages which have been granted in the financial year just drawing to a close alone amounting to nearly £106,000.

" If our men are dissatisfied with the conditions of their employment they have, as you are aware, machinery for representing their views—I venture to say the like of which no other Government Department or private employer has in existence —which secures to them the greatest liberty in the presentation of their case, and its most thorough consideration. Certain improvements in that machinery were introduced in the replies to petitions issued last year, which I hope will render it even more efficient than in the past. To its thoroughness I myself can bear witness, for I myself received no less than 454 deputations in connexion with last year's representations, not the least pleasant of which was the occasion on which I met you this time last year.

" That is the position with regard to your request that we should set aside the skilled labourer and organize as a private yard."

APPENDIX B

DUTIES AND PAY OF RURAL POSTMEN

THE following extracts from the evidence laid before Raikes Committee in 1891, illustrate the conditions of rural postmen's work and the pay they received for it.

Page. 153. " The rural postman from Halesowen to Bromley makes two journeys a day and walks over very hilly ground. His official walk is 16½ miles on week days only, but in order to save the expense of housing himself at the end of his walk, between 10 a.m. and 5.10 p.m., he walks home after completing his first journey by a short cut, and thus walks five miles more a day, or 21½ miles in all. He is unable to get work at the terminal point of his walk, and in any case would be too tired to do much. His wages are 17s. a week, and although he has given 10 years' good service he has not received any good conduct stripes. The parcels he carries add much to his work. He comes on duty at 6.10 a.m. and finishes at 6.15 p.m. He thinks his wages too low, and does not see why he should be paid less than the town postman at Halesowen, viz. 18s.—1s.—22s. a week. His rent is 3s. 2d. a week, and he gets a small house of four rooms."

Page 168. " As an illustration of the duties and

pay of the rural postman I give the following particulars of the case of the Shrewsbury and Yorkton
postman.   His walk is 18½ miles six days a week.
His wages are 15s. a week.   His hours of work as
follows, viz. :

" Attends at Shrewsbury Office at   ..   5.15 a.m.
Reaches end of walk (12½ miles) at..   9.30 a.m.
Starts on return journey at   ..   4.50 p.m.
Reaches Shrewsbury Office at   ..   7.12 p.m.

" He has to pay 1s. a week for housing while
waiting at the end of his walk, and he cannot do work
there because he is too tired.   He has the expense
of getting his dinner away from home."

Page 170.   " I took evidence from two rural
postmen who start from Limerick, and proceed to
give the following particulars relating to the walk to
Ballysimon :

" Attends at Head Office   ..   ..   5.40 a.m.
Reaches Ballysimon   ..   ..   9.30 a.m.
Leaves Ballysimon   ..   ..   6.20 p.m.
Reaches Head Office   ..   ..   7.30 p.m.

" Length of walk 15 miles, 7 days.   Wage 14s. a
week, with a substitute every other Sunday."

Page 175.   Two sub-office postmen (at Southport)
do a full day's work at 14s. 6d. and 15s. respectively.

APPENDIX C

TREASURY OMNIPOTENCE

THE letters here reproduced illustrate the relations between employing Departments and the Treasury. The first—a letter from the Treasury to the Postmaster-General—is taken from the Report of the Fawcett Inquiry (1881) ; and the second is an apologetic letter from Mr. H. C. Raikes (Postmaster-General in 1891) submitting wage proposals which involved higher expenditure. This is included in the Report of the Raikes Inquiry (1891).

The Secretary to the Treasury to the Postmaster-General.

SIR,
    In reply to your letter of the 13th instant, following several personal conferences between yourself and representatives of the Treasury with the assistance of officers from your own Department, I am directed by My Lords to state that they accept the proposals which you submit to them in that letter for improving the pay and general position of the Telegraphists and the Sorting Clerks employed in the service of the Post Office in London and in the country, with the understanding that effect is to be given to the new classification and to the new scale of wages from the 1st of April, 1881, as fast as they

can, with due consideration, be applied to the several offices. These proposals include :

I. A new classification and scale of wages, which is to be uniform for the Postal Staff of the Sorting Branch and for the Telegraphists, involving an increased immediate charge of nearly £44,000, and an increased average charge of £128,000 per annum, as soon as the new rates advance to their normal limits.

II. The cost of the reduction of night attendance to seven hours, involving an increase of more than £9,000 per annum.

III. Improvements in the rate of payment for overtime, and particularly in respect of allowing it on Sundays, Christmas Day, and Good Friday, involving an increase of more than £15,000 per annum.

The joint effect, therefore, of these measures is to increase the cost of the Postal and Telegraph Service at once by £67,000, and prospectively by £152,000 (on an average) per annum.

The amount of this increase of the public charge is quite sufficient of itself to explain the hesitation which My Lords have felt in consenting to it ; nor can they shut their eyes to the means by which the claims for this improvement in the terms of service have been urged upon the Government by a part of the officers interested.

Admitting, as My Lords do, that when discontent is shown to prevail extensively in any branch of the Public Service it calls for attention and inquiry, and, so far as it is proved to be well founded, for redress, they are not prepared to acquiesce in any organized agitation which openly seeks to bring its extensive voting power to bear on the House of Commons against the Executive Government responsible for conducting in detail the administration of the country. The persons who are affected by the changes now proposed are, as you observe, no fewer than 10,000, and the entire Postal Service numbers nearly five times as many. Other branches of the Civil Service employed (and voting) in various parts of the United Kingdom are at least as numerous in the aggregate as the servants of the Post Office. All this vast number of persons, not living like soldiers and sailors outside ordinary civil life, are individually and collectively interested in using their votes to increase in their own favour, the public expenditure, which the rest of the community, who have to gain their living in the unrestricted competition of the open market, must provide by taxation, if it is provided at all.

My Lords, therefore, reserve to themselves the power of directing that the execution of the terms agreed to in the preceding part of this letter be suspended in any post office of which the members are henceforth known to be taking part in extra-official agitation.

They understand that you are inquiring whether the law, as declared in the existing Post Office Acts, does not afford to the public similar protection in respect of postal communication, including telegraphs, as is afforded by the Act 38 and 39 Vict., c. 86, s. 4, to municipal authorities and their contractors against breaches of contracts of service in respect of gas or water, the wilful interruption to the use of which is hardly of more serious import to the local community than is that of postal communication to the national community.

If the existing Post Office Acts do not meet this case, it will be for My Lords to consider whether the circumstances continue to be such as to make it their duty to propose to Parliament an extension to the Post Office of provisions similar to those cited above from the Act 38 and 39 Vict., c. 86.

.   .   .   .

(Signed) F. CAVENDISH.
The Right Hon. Henry Fawcett, M.P.

The Postmaster-General to the Lords of the Treasury.

G.P.O., 13th May, 1891.

MY LORDS,

I am under the necessity of submitting for your Lordships' consideration a large and important measure having for its object a general improvement in the condition of the postmen throughout the United Kingdom.

In the course of last year head-quarters were inundated with postmen's memorials. These memorials . . . coming as they did from every part of the country and preferring various and sometimes conflicting requests, appeared to me to be the outcome, not so much of concerted action as of general discontent; and rather than attempt to deal with the case of each town separately, I determined to appoint a Committee to inquire into the condition of the postmen generally.

Upon this Committee your Lordships were good enough, in pursuance of a comparatively new practice, to allow a member of your Lordships' own Department to serve. . . .

Of the Committee's report, . . . I think I may fairly say that it appears to me an honest and carefully elaborated endeavour to solve a difficult problem. There are some points, however, on which I do not agree with the Committee, and as the simplest mode of dealing with the case I propose to state what these points are, begging your Lordships will understand that those parts of the report in respect to which I do not express disagreement have my full concurrence :

I. London Postmen.

The Committee recommend that the telegraph messengers, on becoming superannuated as such, should be appointed not (as now) to be postmen in London, but to be postmen in the country in the room of a corresponding number of country postmen transferred to London. In theory this may be proper enough, but in practice I am disposed to doubt whether, except perhaps in semi-suburban towns, the inclination on the part of country postmen to be transferred to London would be sufficiently general to afford room for the messengers' absorption. Be that as it may, however, a preferable course, as it appears to me, will be to alter not so much the force from which the London postmen are recruited as the manner in which that force is trained ; and regarding the Army as the best possible school for promoting habits of obedience and smartness of appearance, it is my intention to inaugurate a system by which telegraph messengers, on reaching the age of 18 will be encouraged to enlist in the Army, by the promise that, after five years' military service, they will be appointed postmen if they bring back with them good characters.

On this point, on which I may observe the Secretary of State for War is in complete accord with myself, it would not be necessary to trouble your Lordships were it not that, as part of the system, I propose that so far as wages are concerned, one half of the military service should count as service in the Post Office ; that is to say, that a telegraph messenger who should become a postman after five years' service with the colours should be entitled to enter the postmen's scale not at the minimum, but by two increments in advance and to count six months towards his next increment. Service of slightly more or slightly less than five years with the colours would of course be reckoned in the same proportion.

Accordingly, I request your Lordships to authorize when arranging details with Mr. Secretary Stanhope, to make this a condition of the new system.

.   .   .   .

IV. Country Town Postmen and Rural Postmen.

The courage and liberality which distinguished the Committee elsewhere in their report appear to me to have deserted them here. No scale, in my opinion, should begin for country town postmen as low as 13s., or for rural postmen as low as 12s. Under both heads I propose that the seventh or last of the Committee's scales be struck out, leaving the lowest scale for country town postmen, 15s.—1s.—20s., and the lowest scale for rural postmen, 13s.—1s.—17s.

.   .   .   .

According to the Committee the cost of their proposals, calculated at the mean, will be £129,900 a year. Assuming this estimate to be correct—and I have no reason to doubt it—the cost of the proposals as now modified will, similarly calculated, be £125,650 a year.

Even so, the cost is heavy, far heavier than I care to have to ask your Lordships to authorize ; and yet I feel constrained to do so by the conviction that nothing less will suffice to remove just cause for complaint and place the body of postmen throughout the Kingdom on a sound and satisfactory footing.

.   .   .   .

(Signed) H. C. RAIKES

INDEX

A

" Age " pay, 119, 124, 135
Aircraft Factory. *See* Farn-
    borough
American wages, 92, 158, 159,
    160
Apprenticeship, 46, 47, 65, 102,
    174, 175, 186, 188, 189
Arbitration, 55, 129, 130, 133,
    134, 136, 137, 140, 149,
    151, 153
Board, Civil Service, 129,
    130, 133, 148, 150, 151
Army Ordnance Departments'
    Employees' Union, 10
A.S.E. (A.E.U.), 14, 51, 144
Assistant clerks, 66, 74, 76, 84,
    86
Atlantic mails, 92
Australia, 152, 153, 154, 157,
    158, 160, 168
Austria, 152, 155

B

Bargain. *See* Collective bar-
    gaining
Belgium, 156
Board of Agriculture, 78, 87
    of Trade, 77
Boatswain's gang, 19, 176, 177,
    178, 184
Boilermakers, 44, 47, 172, 174
Bonuses. *See* Wages
Boy labour, 84, 96, 103

C

Caulkers, 29, 42, 44, 46, 47, 187
Charge-pay, 39

Chatham, 29, 35, 41, 51, 52, 59,
    173, 179, 180, 186
Christmas boxes, 91
Civil Service Commissioners, 65
Civil Service Confederation, 146
Clothing factory. *See* Pimlico
Collective bargaining, xx, 27,
    33, 54, 85, 86, 90, 123,
    126, 127, 129, 130, 131,
    134, 137, 146, 147, 150,
    156, 160, 161, 168, 198,
    199
Colonial telegraph services, 92
Combination Acts, xvii
Committee on production, 130,
    131, 133
Competition, 6, 68, 87, 92, 126,
    160, 161
Confined space allowance, 57
Contractors, 7, 37, 41, 55, 169,
    177, 184
Contracts, 3, 4, 45, 123, 127
Continuity. *See* Security
Coppersmiths, 44
Cost of living, 10, 13, 97, 99,
    124, 126, 127
Counter clerks, 117, 124
Crane-drivers, 43, 48, 51

D

Danger money, 57
Deductions, 56, 104, 161
Demarcation, 31, 74
Democratic control, xiv, xvii,
    123
Departmental councils, 138, 142,
    146
Devonport, 28, 29, 30, 41, 54,
    59, 179, 186
Dilution, 131, 132

Diplomatic Service, 79, 156
Dismissals, 16, 21, 58, 177, 187
District rates, xv, xix, 13, 14, 22, 55, 60
Draughtsmen, 78, 87
Drillers, 42, 47, 176

E

Education, 64, 66
Efficiency bars, 127, 169
Electricians, 78
Employees, numbers of, xiii, xiv, 63
Enfield. *See* Waltham and Enfield
Engineers, 9, 13, 40, 41, 42, 47, 59, 86, 183, 189
Establishment. *See* Privileges and Unestablished workers

F

Factory Acts, xvii
    inspectors, 66
Fair Wages Resolution, xv, xix, 1, 10, 12, 40, 60, 166, 170
Family wage. *See* Wages
Farnborough, 13, 14
" Feed and speed," 14, 15, 22
First division clerks, 64, 70, 71, 74, 75
Fitters, electrical, 32
Foremen. *See* Supervisors
France, 154, 156, 157

G

Geddes committee, 24, 25
Germany, 152, 155
Good conduct stripes, 118
Graded offices, 70, 74

H

Haulbowline, 54, 55
Health insurance, 11, 53
Health Insurance Commissions, 70
Holland, 155, 157

Horse-shoes, 6
Hours, 35, 50, 56, 82, 94, 112, 113, 114, 177, 194, 195

I

Imperial penny post, 89
Industrial Court, 55, 141
Inspectors (women), 80
Inter-Departmental Committee, 10, 11, 146
Interim rate, 22
Irish Land Commission. *See* Land Commission
Irish L.G.B. *See* L.G.B.
Italy, 155

J

Joiners, 35, 49, 50
Joint Industrial Councils. *See* Whitley Councils

L

Labour pressure, 1, 8, 11, 14, 119, 120, 132, 144, 159, 166, 197. *See also* Parliamentary agitation
Labour Protection League, 19
Labourers, 8, 9, 13, 19, 20, 21, 35, 40, 44, 50, 55, 191
Land Commission (Ireland), 73, 75, 76
Learners. *See* Apprenticeship
L.G.B., 67, 74, 82
    (Ireland), 72, 74, 82

M

Mail boats, 92
Market demand, xix
    price, 66, 67, 68, 86, 92, 100, 101, 157, 160
Mechanics. *See* Engineers
Medical attendance, 22
    inspectors, 67, 82
Messengers, 83
    boy, 93, 116
Mines Regulations Act, xvii
Minimum wage. *See* Wages

Ministry of Labour, 32
Mint, 86
Monopolist characteristics, xviii, 69, 76, 79, 96, 97, 127, 160
Munitions, 129, 130
Museum service, 74

N

Night work, 94
Nine Hours Act, xvii

O

Office of Works, xvii, 78, 130
Ordnance factories, 14
Output, xix, 25, 168
Overhead charges, 4, 6, 7, 79
Overseers. See Supervisors
Overtime, 50, 96, 112, 113, 197

P

Parliamentary agitation, 6, 37, 39, 45, 120, 121, 122, 123, 127, 166, 169, 197, 198
control, xiv, xv, xvi, 55, 87
Patronage, 63
Patternmakers, 44, 172
Payment by results, 25, 26, 93, 128, 132, 174
Pembroke, 29, 34, 59, 186
Pensions. See Privileges
Pensioners, 104
Petitions, 1, 28, 29, 54, 175, 178, 186, 199
Piecework, 14, 16, 17, 24, 29, 30, 35, 36, 48, 51, 54, 127, 172, 181
Pimlico, 8, 11
Platers, 44
Porters, 8
Portsmouth, 28, 41, 50, 58, 59, 179, 186
Postmaster-General :
and Treasury, xvi
and labour agitation, 121, 122, 123, 124, 148, 197
Postmen, 91, 100, 107, 111, 126, 127, 136, 199, 200, 201, 202
Postmen's walks, 114, 194, 195
Post Office revenue, 89, 90

Post Office schedule, 93, 97, 109
Postwomen, 136
Premium bonus, 14, 33, 39, 172, 173
Price-fixing, 14, 16, 23, 24, 54
Private employment, 7, 25, 27, 29, 36, 38, 45, 46, 49, 66, 69, 85, 119, 125, 160, 161, 162, 163, 166, 169, 177, 182, 183, 184, 190
Privileges (pensions, etc.), 1, 11, 12, 21, 22, 36, 51, 52, 53, 68, 73, 88, 105, 117, 160, 161, 169, 178, 186
Promotion, 72, 73

R

Rate-cutting, 16, 17, 25, 35, 104, 105, 107, 108, 114, 165
Rate-fixing, 16, 17
Real wages. See Wages
Recruiting, 63, 64, 65, 69
Registrar-General, 69, 70, 71
Riggers, 35, 51
Risk money, 35
Riveters, 29, 42, 44, 46, 47, 179
Rosyth, 59
Rural postmen, 99, 114, 115, 116, 124, 125, 127, 194, 201

S

Sailmakers, 40, 44
Second Division clerks, 64, 71, 72, 73, 74, 75, 85, 96, 103
Security and continuity, xix, 58, 68, 152, 164, 168, 170, 173, 177
Sheerness, 32, 35, 186
Shipwrights, 34, 44, 48, 59, 176
Shop stewards, 23
Shorthand writers, 67, 82
Sick pay. See Privileges
Skilled labourers, 18, 19, 20, 30, 35, 36, 39, 42, 43, 44, 45, 46, 47, 50, 51, 55, 172, 173, 174, 175, 176, 178, 179, 180, 181, 182, 184, 185, 186, 188, 189, 191, 192
Slow workers, 16, 22

Small Arms factory. *See* Waltham and Enfield
Solicitors, 77
Sorters, 96, 102, 111, 112
Sorting clerks and telegraphists, 92, 95, 98, 102, 103, 104, 111, 124, 196, 197
Sovereignty, xv, xvi, xx, 28, 129, 150, 151, 168, 169
Speeding up, 105
Split duties, 111, 112
Staff officers, 71, 72, 73
Storehouse clerks, 19, 21
  men, 8
Strikes, 23, 41, 60
Substitution duty, 96, 103, 110, 127
Supervisors, 3, 4, 5, 6, 119, 124
Supplementary clerks, 71, 72
Supply and demand, xix, xx, 46, 65, 85, 91, 163, 164, 171, 188
Surveyors, 73, 135

T

Tailoresses, 8
Telegraphists. *See* Sorting clerks and telegraphists
Telephonists, 105
Temporary workers. *See* Unestablished workers
Time rates, 14, 48
Trade councils, 138
  Union Congress, 11, 12, 15, 33, 45, 172, 174, 181
  Union rates, 38, 40, 45, 48
  Unions Act, xvii
Travelling post offices, 112
Treasury control, xiv, xvi, xix, xx, 21, 25, 51, 67, 70, 74, 81, 83, 85, 106, 123, 138, 140, 141, 145, 149, 164, 165, 166, 169, 196
Typists, 81, 135

U

Unestablished workers, 63, 68, 69, 76, 77, 78, 79, 82, 88, 103, 105, 106, 107, 108, 127, 135, 178

Unit Schedule. *See* Post Office schedule

V

Vested interests, 19, 124

W

Wages :
  Basis of, xviii, 91, 115, 126, 136, 168, 171
  Bonuses, 133, 134
  Deductions, 23
  Family, 81, 157
  In private employment, xix, 2
  Legislation, xvii, xviii
  Living, 14, 66, 76, 87, 96, 99, 101, 135, 154, 157, 160
  Minimum, 8, 10, 13, 38, 39, 41, 43, 46, 66, 86
  " Prescribed," 30, 31
  Rates, 2, 66, 72, 73, 74, 76, 77, 81, 82, 83, 86, 92, 95, 102, 103, 114, 115, 116, 124, 133, 172, 174, 175, 180, 186, 192, 194, 195, 201
  Real, 98, 99, 100, 130, 134, 135, 136, 158
  Theory of, xviii
  Unskilled men's, 130
  Women's, 80, 113, 114, 130, 131, 132, 136, 157
Waltham and Enfield, 2, 9
War Cabinet, 138, 147
Weedon, 10, 11
Whitley Committee, 137, 138, 141, 142, 143
Whitley Councils, 24, 31, 55, 86, 127, 134, 137, 140, 142, 143, 144, 146, 147, 148, 149, 150, 151
Woolwich Arsenal, 2, 3, 4, 5, 6, 7, 9, 14, 16, 17, 18, 19, 22, 23, 24, 142

Workers :
    Numbers of. *See* Employees
    Weaknesses of, xx
    Women, 80, 81, 84, 96, 100, 102, 113, 157
Workmen's Compensation, 32, 53
Works Loan Board, 77

Y

Yard officers, 44

Z

Zones (London), 91, 100, 109, 110

For Product Safety Concerns and Information please contact our
EU representative GPSR@taylorandfrancis.com Taylor & Francis
Verlag GmbH, Kaufingerstraße 24, 80331 München, Germany